God's Radiance

Lana 'LJ' Joseph

inner child press, ltd

Credits

Author
Lana 'LJ' Joseph

Editor
hülya n. yılmaz, Ph.D.

Cover Design
William S. Peters, Sr.
&
Inner Child Press, Ltd.

Disclaimer from the Editing Department

Editing is not the exact science one would expect. Many times, when considering and employing the rules of English upon a creative work, the authenticity of the authors' words and meaning can be lost. This outcome applies to the writings with a dialectal, colloquial or eclectic style, in particular. Sometimes this loss can be profound and deprive the reader of the genuine aspects of the writers' thoughts, feelings and innate flavor. At Inner Child Press International, we honor and respect each author's unique creativity, and we strive to maintain the integrity of their offerings. This approach may include such nuances as capitalization, punctuation and other standard rules of grammar.

hülya n. yılmaz, Ph.D.
Director of Editing Services

General Information

God's Radiance
Lana 'LJ' Joseph

1st Edition: 2020

This publishing is protected under Copyright Law as a "Collection". All rights for all submissions are retained by the individual author and / or artist. No part of this publishing may be reproduced, transferred in any manner without the prior **WRITTEN CONSENT** of the "Material Owner" or its representative Inner Child Press, ltd. Any such violation infringes upon the creative and intellectual property of the owner pursuant to International and Federal Copyright Law. Any queries pertaining to this "Collection" should be addressed to Publisher of Record.

Publisher Information

1st Edition: Inner Child Press
intouch@innerchildpress.com
www.innerchildpress.com

This Collection is protected under U.S. and International Copyright Laws

ISBN-13: 978-1-952081-01-9 (inner child press, ltd.)

$ 19.95

Dedicated to

My beloved parents, Michael Sims Jones Sr. and Delores W. Wilson (Jones) Norris, who always showed me unconditional love;

My Pops, Felix A. Norris, who has been a father figure role model since the transition of my beloved father;

My beautiful circle of family, extended family and poesy family, that continues to humble me and help me soar beyond this galaxy;

My loves and heartbeats: Christopher, Willie, Michaela, Quinn and Devonte, my children & bonus children who give me a reason to be the best human being that I can be here on Earth;

My nephews, nieces, great nephews and great nieces, who make me proud to be an Auntie;

Finally, to my beloved husband, King "Artist" Rodney Dion Smith, the one and only one hue-man who promised to heal me with his love, and did.

Table of Contents

Preface xv

The Poetry

I Want My Poetry to . . .	3
The Power of Unity	7
Lavender Scars	8
Stronger Than You Know	9
Bonds That Bind	12
Black Girl / Queen / Me	13
Enraged	18
Adorned Freedom	21
God Called You Home	22
She Speaks Ascension	23
Gifts	25
Sage	27
Faces in the Crowd	28
Child's EyE	29
The Purple Flow	31
Mirrored Illusions	32

Table of Contents... *continued*

tasting eXtraordinary . . .	34
Blue Power	35
This 'Ish	36
Essence & Remix	39
Showers of Blessings	42
Beyond the Veil	44
Senses	45
The Matriarch	46
You Remind Me of Mama's Garden	47
From Sunrise to Sunset	49
When You Awaken Tomorrow . . .	51
The Hand of Time	53
Out of the Shadows	55
My Homage to All Queens & Queen Mothers	56
Blue Sliding Doors	57
Nubian Queens	59
Beloved Prince	60
Ageing	62
A Child Rose	64
Quietly . . .	66

Table of Contents ... *continued*

Love Now!	67
Red Rain	68
Rise	69
Immovable	70
Irrelevant	71
I Live Here	72
Moment to Moment	73
Gratitude	75
Black Pearls	76
I'm Tied . . .	77
A Dream, Realized	78
Shadow & Death (No Masterpiece!)	79
Love Without Wings	85
All Blessings Are Good to Me	86
Chilled	88
A Jazzy Good Time	90
A Love-Letter	91
Rings	92
God's Babes	93
U-N-I-T-Y	94
The Scribe in Me	95

Table of Contents... *continued*

Organic Love	96
The Innocent	97
The Beauty of Nature	98
Shine On!	99
I / EyE Love Nature	101
golden chocolate	102
Earth-Days	103
self-love	104
Purple Love	105
Here EyE Stand	106
Always 1 God, 1 Love	107
What If?	108
Glory	109
Blessed to Connect	110
What Makes My Life Sparkle . . .	111
Uncensored Thoughts	112
Will You Catch Me as I Fall?	113
Why I Write	114
Love and Happiness Is . . .	116
Macroscopic Thoughts	118
Looking out of the Window . . . Waiting . . .	120

Table of Contents ... *continued*

Shining Beyond the Blues	123
Will You Unmask You?	124
Black Roses	126
i want . . .	127
Togetherness	128
I'm in Love	129
I Will Never Forget!	131
The Ebony King	133
Angels in Unusual Places	137
Raven's Love-Letter	139
A Double Rainbow	141
Let Go!	142
Your Strength Lies Within	144
If Only . . .	146
Strength & Determination	148
To Live a Life Full of PEACE and JOY	150
In Silence	151
My Soulmate	152
The Climate Change	154
my beloved mommy	156
Poetic Blossoms	157

Table of Contents... *continued*

My Hero	158
A Legacy of Queen Matriarchs	159
Dedicated to My Ebony Queens	160
Truth	161
Tranquility	162
My Love for Thee	163
Praying...	164
Breaking the Rules...	165
Technical Difficulties	167
A Love & Peace-Prayer	169
The Warrior Queen...	170
Beyond Illness	171
my crown	173
dare to listen to your own muse~ic	174
For My Ancestors	176
Scattered	177
When I Found You...	179
The Phenomenal One	180
Brevity	181
Ode to the Godfather of Soul	182
No Need to Shovel the Sunrise!	183

Table of Contents . . . *continued*

That Place Within a Journey	185
I'm a Natural Born Libra	186
first kisses	187
A Celebration	188
the brightly-lit light in their eyes	189
Just Me . . . Queen aka Lana "LJ" Joseph	191
Loving ME	193
God's Radiance	194

Author's Quotes & Haiku-Poems — 197

Epilogue	215
About the Author	217

reface

"LJ" is the pseudonym I use in my written work. For several reasons, I have chosen to remain anonymous on public platforms. Specifically, for the purpose of separating my artistic world from my personal environments. I was blessed with a scholarship to have my first book published. I am grateful and thankful for my phenomenal and extraordinary publisher, William S. Peters Sr. He is truly a divine gift from our Creator. Additionally, I am very grateful for this opportunity to share my gifts from God.

In addition, I would like to thank everyone in the world who has embraced me and my literary works. I tend to always write for myself and the heir of my soul. It is such a great honor and pleasure to have my creative offerings well-received by audiences of all ages, socioeconomic background and different cultures. Humbly, I thank you all for blessing me with your beautiful souls.

Lana 'LJ' Joseph

God's Radiance

Lana 'LJ' Joseph

The Poetry

God's Radiance

I Want My Poetry to . . .

I want my poetry to be an epic literary piece of soulful art,
with a generous supply of rhythm.
Poetically, I want to breathe life into the lifeless,
isolated and brokenhearted.

I want my poetry to add relevance
to sleeping and weeping souls;
especially to those who have given up hope.
Passionately, I support those who trust God.
I stand as a bridge for life, love, faith, unity and peace.
Truth speaks through my shadowy cries of golden verses.

I want my poetry to help change the world
by making a positive difference to the human race.
I want my love for literature and language to resonate
beyond the surface areas of life
through our spiritual realm,
My hope is to reach youth and adults.
Happiness grows from within . . .
that special place where God resides.

I want my poetry to be liberating,
bringing peace to mindsets drenched in uneasiness;
unmasking soiled veils stained in purple red rain,
empowering and inspiring beautiful spirits.

I want my poetry to scribe a permanent space
in the hearts and souls of the masses.
I want to leave a legacy of love for all God's children,
while poetically kissing souls through poesy.
I honor beloved kings and queens;
I honor gods and goddesses;
I embrace oneness as my family.

God's Radiance

What I hope to achieve with my poetry
is perhaps a mystery and a bit grandiose.
But for human beings feeling trapped inside
and beautiful souls uplifting people all the time,
my prayer is for opportunities to shine my lit light;
And to sign my name into hearts and spirits –
loving souls beyond nationalities, cultures
and socioeconomic statuses.

These things I have shared are vital
to the core of my very being.
These expectations I put forth into the universe
are what I want my poetry to do.

The Power of Unity

As a very young child,
I was taught many things;
I learned many clichés,
one was "United we stand, divided we fall."
This way of thinking was like our family motto.
I grew to know this is more than a cliché;
it is a true statement.
Additionally, my elders spoke about FAMILY & UNITY.
Those two powerful words went hand in hand.
I am grateful for my parents and other elders in my family.
They taught my siblings and me the importance of
working together, praying together, assisting each other
and standing together . . .
Whenever one of us deviated from our UNITED front,
there were always negative outcomes.

Today, there is still power in UNITY!
I am on bent knees praying . . .
I am praying for awakenings . . .
I am praying for true understanding . . .
STRENGTH comes from UNITY,
and WEAKNESS comes from DIVISION!
Let's refuse to be DIVIDED
and STAND as ONE UNITED PEOPLE!

Lavender Scars

she trusted you
her lavender blues
sunshine hues
peering through between rays of smoke-filled clouds
rain . . .
possibly in the forecast
she welcomes you
hues of blues . . .
flashing lights
downpour . . .
pouring down
hoping to catch a glimpse of fear
perhaps just waiting for streams of tears
or a reason to disrupt serenity
lying beneath melanin skin
within . . .
rapid heart-beats, soul screams
softly, she surrendered smiles
through years of wrinkled cheek bones
hiding lavender scars
perhaps it would only make a difference to those who knew her?
perhaps it would make no difference at all?
perhaps this time will be different?

Stronger Than You Know

Beloved King . . . you see . . . and over-see . . .
You mean so much to me . . . and to many
of those who know you,
who may not have expressed it . . .
lately
but . . .
you are a remarkable divine gift.

I wonder if you realize . . .
you are stronger than you know?
You have evolved.
You're
a gallant great man
a leader warrior soldier
a fearless best friend
a scintillating boyfriend
a devoted groom to-be
a divine faithful husband
a genuine steadfast brother
a thoughtful patient uncle
a marvelous inquisitive nephew
a spectacular vivacious cousin
and so much more . . .

To your family,
you are hope and faith.
You are their shining light.
You make the family work.
You worship and praise God every day,
and everything turns out alright.

I'm not sure if you've heard it lately,
but I'd like to shout it out thunderously . . .
you are stronger than you know!
Not only are you revered
for having a loving spiritual character
but also, for being such a respectable phenomenal father
and a bona-fide Daddy.

Your children are truly blessed to have you.
You possess the qualities of a godly man . . .
one who leads by showing unconditional love & faith.
You're an exceptional example of a Dad . . .
You teach your children to be reverent in behavior,
and your family continues to rejoice in gratitude
for your divine earthly being.

You are loved, adored and appreciated
to all those who know you well.
Dependability is another attribute that you've always held.
Sincerity and reliability are character traits you daily wear,
just as your humbleness . . .
which is evident to all those who remain aware.
Additionally,
you give freely to those less fortunate.
Without a blink of an eye, you do your best to assist.
Please know . . .
you have made a huge difference in the lives of our sisters and brothers.
Our Heavenly Master saw you turn no blind eye.

Quality
is what you are . . . standing tall . . . representing a real leader.
Beloved King . . . keep the dream alive . . .
continue raising leaders . . .
Boys and girls equally
need to understand true examples of leadership characteristics.
Knowing you is like wearing a sacred badge of honor.
Through the difficult times you still shine.
You remain armed and suited up . . . with unwavering Man-Power.
I am very proud of you.
You are stronger than you know . . .
Yes, you show your strength with your beautiful brilliant Mastermind.
I believe our heavenly Master has Angels here on earth . . .
watching over you and guiding you through and through.

Every step you take,
every decision you make
are all part of His monumental plan.
Beautiful watchers and keepers of your precious sacred spirit
are also sent-in living angel beings . . .
Spiritually celestial ones are helping to guide you here on earth.

Yes . . .
ever since your birth.

Gentle-man . . .
you are without a doubt.
As history often times
repeats itself . . .
you are like your father.

You exude courage
from your gentle strong soul.
What a blessing it is to have the privilege to know
YOU
and to know that in this universe . . .
there are other like-minded creative souls
that share honorable characteristics . . .
and a royal swag like yours.

I need you to feel me . . .
While you're filling all of your responsible manly deeds,
understand me, beloved King . . .
as I'm doing my best to express from within the depths of my soul . . .
that YOU . . .
yes,
YOU . . .
are stronger than you know . . .
The little boy that still resides in you . . .
perhaps had to overcome many struggles from early childhood.
However, he is still . . .
bright
adventurous
helpful
and mischievous . . .
with a tough load to carry.

Take time to enjoy a bit of pride in the fruits of your hard labor . . .
sit back and have fun, while tasting divine flavors.
For you have come a long way baby . . .
with a bit more east to go.
Please never forget . . .
You are stronger than you know!

Bonds That Bind

        Sacred
        Ancestors'
        blood
        bled
        for me
    for us
  for
family . . .

    realizing . . . promise
    shedding hope some never knew
    beneath the Heaven

        many stood like trees
        roots were firm . . . like men before
        women strong . . . grounded

          manifesting hope
    love . . . faith . . . kindness . . . dreams realized
          Now . . . what do we breathe?

Are the bonds that bind polluted with hate?
Are we standing tall,
planted and deeply rooted in shades
like men & women who sacrificed for many?

              I believe in love.

I believe that the essence of love is our perception.

If we love and believe in ourselves . . .
we can achieve beyond our dreams.

            When we know
            who came before
            we can do so much more.

      When we are united
      we can be so much more!

Black Girl / Queen / Me

I am still the thin Black Girl within
Who grew up to be
the woman called **Queen**,
ME

Moment to moment I work on myself
A daily spiritual plight
To God I owe my entire life
I thank him for the challenges
No longer asking to remove all strife
I pray for wisdom to keep balances

As a little girl, I was scorned
for wearing my rich black skin
I was hurt
ridiculed
beaten
and called "ugly nigger girl"
by a so-called good friend
Yet,
this flesh was blessed . . .
blessed beyond measure
I had my mother back then
She was a God-given treasure
whom I could talk to whenever
and have a shoulder to lean
She was my heart
My world
My best friend
Her . . .
I still desperately mourn
The loss of my mother
I'm painfully torn
Her departure from this earth . . .
I'll never get over
My bond with mom started at birth

Our Father God is working with me
He's helping me get through it

God's Radiance

I continue holding on . . .
to precious moments adrift
I'm blessed to have my family,
my wonderful dear friends too
and my special BFF . . . who's always true
I cherish them all . . . through and through
And that includes all of **YOU**

I also thank our dear Lord
For blessing me with a career I loved
Every little boy and girl, I truly adored
Teaching God's precious children
was like living in a dream world

Time has passed now,
many things have turned upside down
But what the enemy meant for my destruction
Our Master gave blessings abundance

I've learned a long time ago
That people don't always say what they mean

BLACK GIRL
QUEEN
ME

I say what I mean.
I mean what I say
I do what I mean
I do what I say
When I love you
I tell you

I show you with my actions
Because I love you

"Speak your mind freely" some will say
"You can always come to me"
Unfortunately, in the past
I did go to them . . . and . . .
they proved not to be a friend
Friendships did not last

Many turned their back
When the road got tough
They left with their words . . .
that didn't mean very much

Forgiveness is how I live
I've kept them in my prayers
While giving all issues to Him

I'm working on myself each day
Studying how to please God
Learning how to be still
I try my very best
to serve humanity

Yesss . . .
there are times
I fall short of my goal
I'm striving though
To be the best woman I can
For our Father God to know

This
BLACK GIRL
QUEEN
ME

Continuously . . .
I'm being judged by many
Even though God said,
Profoundly
In Matthew 7:1,
"Judge ye not, that ye not be judged."

I grew up hearing all sorts of scriptures
Phrases
Statements
Songs
Praises
Pertaining to God
And people's wrongs
But . . .

God's Radiance

He without sin let him cast the first stone
Some things I will never understand
So, I try to remember what Jesus said
In Proverbs 3:5,
"Trust in the Lord with all thine heart
and lean not unto thine own understanding."

My only purpose in this life as I know it
Is to continue doing the Master's work
and keep assisting my fellow man
In any way that I can

I believe that God has given me the gift of a Poet
But even that is to be used
Never abused
And I do know it

I grew to love this
Black girl
That resides in me
I've grown to appreciate and love
my chocolate bronze tone
There's no pretense to be shown

My family and true friends love me
I am comfortable in my own skin
The hatred I experienced was way back then
And I do not allow it to bother me now
I keep no negative thoughts
There are people that just cannot
embrace me because I'm Black

I pray for those who hate and despise me
I pray for anyone in this earth or our society
That will not allow me to share my love
because they hate my brown skin tone
given to me from our Master above
I will still leave this earth happy
My soul is smiling right now
I refuse to wear a frown
Because God loves

This . . .
BLACK GIRL
QUEEN
ME

Enraged

I rage the rage of a mad person,
holding a Twelve-Gage.
I rage because every time
I turn on the TV or computer
or turn a newspaper page,
I see more than 15 of my melanin
brothas' and sistas' names
dead . . .
The obituaries cannot fully hold
the names of all these stars.
Why?
Because you will not find them
in the entertainment section.
You will not find them listed
in the food section
or successful-story headlines.
We are dying!!!
Why do we keep singing this same
sad song?
In the words of one of our beloveds,
Brotha King Marvin Gaye,
"What's Going On?"
This 'ish has been happening
waaay toooo looooong!!!
I have family & friends
and friends of friends
in many walks of society
who have made their life's purpose
a high priority.
Yet,
they do not hear these cries
for them.
Their world is bling bling
for the mothers and fathers
whose children are slain.
Their tears water the ground with pain.
Their deepest fears are realized.
I sigh.
I cry.

Lana Joseph

I am ENRAGED!
When one of our children leave
this planet untimely . . .
it feels as though our life's breath
is literally placed on a vacuum's
highest setting.
Imagine a vacuum sealed to your mouth
and turned on high for 2 minutes
before you can scream or gasp for air.
That is the way it feels
when the murders of our melanin children
are broadcast on TV or radio.
Is that all we have are prayers?
I rage when I hear the headline news say,
an African American baby named Sage
was shot and killed today.
She was 2 years of age.
And what is always stated:
"It's possibly drugs- and gang-related."
And right after that,
the newscaster announces:
"In other news,
the Dow Jones is steadily on an up-trend,
and today will be sunny skies with a high of 74°."
In Entertainment:
"Zack Snyder, Director of Batman VS Superman,
Dawn of Justice,
has a hit film on his hands . . .
opening weekend grossed an astounding
487 Million Dollars."
But,
where is the information
on baby Sage?
RAGE!
Rage . . . is what's being spilled
onto this page
because of the mass genocide of my people
like a beast held captive, tortured and given no food for many days . . .
Or a person who has been on their job for years,
but received no promotion or raise.
Meanwhile,
I see Facebook posts:

"Do not disturb,
I'm watching my favorite show!"
This major hit series, "Walking Dead"
has many in society misled
and some messed up in the head
while our babies are being shot
DEAD!
It seems as though we are the Zombies.
Life is no Reality TV-show
in the real world . . .
Who are the target people?
Whose blood is being shed?
R.I.P. to all of our melanin people
who were just killed today!
These are but only a few examples
of
why
RAGE
is being spilled on this page!

Adorned Freedom

stand natural
grounded as a tree
understanding not

natural fashion
i wear boldly . . . free
no need for blind gifts

no need to change me
God perfected us
beauty . . . and . . . happy
Why give red to me?
i am adorned . . . freedom . . .

God Called You Home

12 years ago, April 18th,
you joined our Heavenly Father.
It was an awfully difficult day for me.
Letting go is never easy.
Loving you was very easy.
I loved you so hard that I wanted you to stay.
I loved you so much I wanted you out of pain.
I came to realize that it was only one way,
one way for my prayers to be answered.
God had to call you home!

I had to let go of your physical temple.
I had to learn to accept your true natural form.
I had to realize that God answered my prayers.
I know that He answered yours too.
No more pain . . .
No more suffering . . .
No more CANCER!
God called you home!

She Speaks Ascension

She speaks with closed eyes . . .
many tears held within
pain could not bend
yet, she holds the sparkle
inside her soul
she stands for more than freedom ringing
she embraces all the wounded souls that could not speak.

She grounds herself within wisdom
hoping her people would dare to peer beneath the layers of brushstrokes
she relishes in the thought that some of her brothers and sisters
would dare to visualize
their dreams and just believe
with every fiber in them.

She hopes for a day that those brave
enough would stop the fight between Him and them
for He is greater than all
if our brothers and sisters would dare
to stand up for what is right and stare
stare at themselves . . .
while gazing upon her stoic ebony beauty
she hopes that the stars without the stripes
would remind them of who they are.

She speaks loudly and clearly through her artistic silence
listen closely and understand that this Truth-Speaking
is directly from a Queen of one true Nation . . .
upon Nations
God's sons are to rise and act as Kings in a land not foreign
we are here as we are meant to be
our choice was made, and through
the womb of ebony Queens,
you, sons were destined to reign as Kings
with royal blood running through your veins.

You have the power to overturn
the wrongs of this Nation
and dare to stand up as a rightful heir

God's Radiance

look the enemies in their blind eyes and stare
do what has to be done to protect your families.

Remember that Love, life and liberty
is your choice . . .
just as happiness is within the God in us.

Look through her and see the change that is necessary
please do not stay stuck on pain
as most wounded Queens . . .
she continues with or without her mate
even though you, sons are the ones to be true leaders and Kings.

True examples, primarily for your Queens . . .
and future Queens and Kings
see me beautiful souls
feel the spirits I hold
stand and be bold.

Be the stars leading in Unity
stop the tears before falling
bless those in the cold
touch the sons of duty.

She speaks to listen . . .
can we touch the tears?
beauty has no fears

she speaks ascension
action divine alfa male.
She is ebony Queen.

*A scribe inspired by the artwork of a phenomenal artist & brother, King Addonis Parker. Thank you so much my beloved brother & King Addonis Parker for always GIFTING your creative & soulful works of genius art to the world! I dedicate this piece to you for ALL of the years that you shared YOU and your God-given gifts & talents worldwide. May God continue to bless you abundantly. I love you. I appreciate you, and I am honored to know you my beloved brother. Blessings Overflowing . . .

Gifts

Gifts are all around me . . .
i take nothing
and no one
for granted!
When i was a child,
birthdays and Christmas
were my favorite days of the year.
Excitement would build
as i looked forward to
gifts to unwrap.
The uncertainty of the contents
brought such a happy feeling.
As i grew older,
i realized that my gifts
were nothing i could unwrap,
sacred gifts of life
God and His divine love . . . Sun
every breath on earth
every time i smell flowers
every sunrise that lights my heart
every sunset that kisses my soul
every chance i see the ocean
everyday i hug my loved ones
everyday i hear laughter
everyday my work is done
everyday i listen to a great musician
everyday i am bitten by love's friction
everyday i taste "i love you" . . .
Every day, i am blessed with gifts . . .
My family,
eXtended family
and friends
are my greatest
and most beloved gifts
here on earth.
The culmination of maturation
and life's experiences
changed my views about gifts.
Gifts surround me daily . . .

God's Radiance

the beautiful souls in my life,
the smell of a newborn baby,
communicating with people,
assisting someone in need,
serving seasoned adults,
treatment for better health,
a roof over my head,
food, clothes, bills paid,
and a warm bed . . .
There are so many things
i consider as gifts that
i am unable to list all now.
However . . .
i take nothing
and no one
for granted!
Everything in our Galaxy holds precious "Gifts".

Sage

A vibrant broken flower
tapered in bitterness

wide-eyed

resting in an icy garden

dreams evaporated
yesterday's
shadowy whole . . .
the aftermath of tomorrow
like spring fruit withered

. . . withered before ripening
sunken to the channel of borrowed breath

severely floundered . . .
. . . unprotected
Sage . . .
bleeds wounded eyes

tears dying . . . passing time's veil

silent screams

Beauty____.

Faces in the Crowd

Resting memories
shadowy visions
quiet days

seasons past
seeing you
your face
facing me

holding hands
embracing time
abstruse plan

sunrise whispers
ingenious queen
hauntingly still

plummeted forward

against odds
firmly rooted
standing keen

She stood out among the faces in a crowd
My Shero.
My advocate.

Child's EyE

Roots
my foundation
strong
lasting
heritage
culture . . .

EyE see strangers
destroying our water
destroying our land
destroying our ancestors' dreams . . .

EyE see strangers
arrive . . . by the dozens
arrive . . . with guns
arrive . . . with unkindness

EyE see unfamiliar . . .
familiar strangers
taking pictures
cameras staged
our tribal paint copied
why?

EyE see productions being made
mothers and sisters being adorned
those are not all original tribal wears
why have strangers put those flowers on her hair?
why are they painting our mothers, brothers and sisters?
why are they altering our native attire and calling it natural?

I sit here . . .
peering out
from my view.

Many things about these strangers
cause me to ponder;
what are their smiling dangers?
Many things about these strangers

God's Radiance

cause me to wonder;
what do they really want?

Quietly
EyE
see why . . .

The Purple Flow

she stood . . . grounded roots
made me think of ancestors
regal . . . walked alone.

some joined hand in hand
royal . . . they were indeed . . . free
some were beaten . . . bruised

the purple flow . . . picked
some 'til the moon lit . . . blood red
remember us . . . first____ .

Mirrored Illusions

You ghost-walked into the frosted background,
peering through purple vein's violet hole;
imprinted upon the opening walls bound,
stood a closed and overexposed veiled door.

Or, was this shadowy frame an illusion forebode?

As yellowed streak-stains embedded the core,
bleached souls rendered colorless to sacred interpretation;
twisted mirrored reflections appeared upon thickened skin . . .

The complexity only exists as nature's unspoiled cave,
washed-away crimson rain, unveiling love's algorithm

Shedding . . . stripping . . . peeling . . . ripping . . .
and tearing stained residue of what once was,
a new dawning and culmination of unraveled souls
Silently . . .
Silenced

As the wind-moving shadow of palms guiding these temples,
gregarious lessons identified through your exhibitions,
blowing faded horrors down-wind

No more yielding to past passions of collecting skulls
No more rising to sunshine-tears carrying darkness
Time's pulse holds God's will
as these tears we shed speak Love
Look now . . .

Do you see the sun in these mirrors?
Listen . . .

Do you hear the unspoiled stream of cries
through contorted mirrored images?
Touch . . .

Do you feel the rumination of this womb-laced prison-bed?
Partake . . .

Do you taste the one-dimensional ego of nothingness?
Speak . . .

Do you choose painted visions
under the castles of blind silent love?

tasting eXtraordinary . . .

She never stopped loving herself
yet,
all of her experiences left her questioning everything she believed in
an awakening like none other transpired.
There were times in her past when she believed her differences were alien
her actions were unorthodox
she always operated against the grain,
the way she handled things caused many to frown upon her
expressing things were unacceptable . . .
only one angelic inspiration embraced her;
that beautiful being made the ultimate earthly transition
she felt excluded from her part of the universe
until she met an amazing group of creatures
those extraordinary beings are called Artists . . .
at last, she was accepted among this group
no longer did she feel alienated
if any part of her was alien,
after tasting extraordinary . . .
she was no longer alone.

Those beautiful souls made her feel home . . .

Blue Power

Where blue shades 'pon trees . . .
they will preserve blood nature
libation change . . . men____
a King's longitude
will affect . . . his latitude
he will indulge not____

romance here . . . is dead
the Congo drums played with red
danced . . . fed . . . false romance____

He is One . . . Only . . .
stay strong, my tribe . . . Father . . . EyEs
Son . . . Holy One . . . Love____

one's tribal power
needs . . . no vices . . . no bribes . . . blue
power held by truth_____ .

This 'Ish

The broken promises
The selfishness
The emptiness
The betrayal
The deceit
The hurt
The pain

Blood . . .
Bled . . .
Bleeding . . .
I turned the other cheek!

I gave . . .
and kept giving.
Giving me . . .
Giving all . . .
Giving freely . . .
Sharing my blessings
Doing my best . . .
to always be a blessing
Thankful to God . . .
for always blessing me.

Selfishly unselfishly . . .
Giving
Knowing all my needs . . .
were cared for.
Hoarding all I have . . . I've never done.
Openly sharing . . . openly caring . . .
Openly loving . . . all . . . in abundance.
Showing . . . not telling.
Willing to let go . . .
Going . . .
Going . . .
Gone!

Selfishly unselfishly . . .
Judging not . . .

just living life happily.
Being tested . . .
Tested . . .
Tested . . .
And still being tested . . .
Testing . . .
Testing . . .
One . . . Two . . . Three . . .
Testing . . .

Is the joke on me . . .
for being who I am,
because I stood . . .
at times when no one else would?
Standing tall . . .
Without demanding . . .
and still withstanding.
Now . . .
I have no understanding.

Sacrificing . . .
I know what that is.

Like Jesus . . . Never will anyone . . . come close.
Yes . . .
I sacrificed . . .
and sacrificed . . .
and . . . sacrificed . . .
And still sacrificing.
Have I sacrificed enough?
I have no count!
The losses are gone . . .

All that I have . . .
all that I am . . .
with all of my being . . .
Gone!
But . . .
When did I sign on to be a martyr?
Excuse me . . . I did not!
Yet . . .
Here I am . . .

God's Radiance

at the bottom of the pit.
Left to rot!

Can I . . .
pull myself . . .
out of this 'ish?

Essence & Remix

Essence

Staring through the black hole of life
Salvaging the essence of my soul
Through explosions falling swiftly
Sharpening blades battling iron paved
Fiery shoots, spurting inwardly

Destroying flighty words
Charging sparks soaring course
Sensing the core's suspension
Locking energies blood spoils
Earth's golden light raining fate
Faithfully gathering tortured sheep
Fleeting emotions slowly wavering
Frozen rainbows' wintry cold peace

Vile and violently attacking honor
Fallen in evil's shadowy lair
Passed judgment where one should not
Foreboding noble hearts and souls to fear
Future seen clearly, piercing in feign eyes
Looking through hallows' rabbit hole
Pain thrown in minds, tormented in binds
Choosing change, not societies' shady mold

Cold blood tomb, piled like layered bricks
Touching silent souls, authentic royal roads
Prisoner of dying minds, seen and unseen tricks
Tasting mirror images and illusions of control

God's Radiance

Remix

As I look at the reality of life,
often times . . .
I witness darkness' overshadowing light
I tighten my divine spiritual armor
and stand on faith
I stay ready to battle life's evils
as I'm being attacked from within
and the day to day bull-ish of 'them'

People have said good things to me,
while in my face, all was going great
When life's situations got rough
Dishonor showed the true person's dirt
Their word was no good
Even my own kin-folk turned on me
No matter . . . No worries . . .
I keep locking out evil and negativity

We were born in a world of light and dark
Sometimes given great opportunities
battling right from wrong & good vs evil
I keep getting knocked down,
and breathing the breaths to survive
Our heavenly Master reigns divine
Through hell's fire, I remain cool
while thanking our Father, for I am no fool
The enemy wants my soul
I make no deals with him
I have given mine to the One Divine

I was lied on, convicted and imprisoned
My reputation and social honor demolished
Those who judged me did not know me
Yet, they destroyed everything I worked for
And dismissed me like a 2-bit whore
I was told that my life was over

Those 'bright' people kept telling me,
I no longer had a future
Even my present was dead, that's what they said

Meanwhile, I kept my trust & faith in God
Moving forward is what I did
Changing to keep my sanity and peace of mind
day by day, ignoring the hateful remarks
I stayed focused on my business grind
refusing to give into sinful crimes
haters and death-eaters already had me buried

Attorneys, Judges and Jury, hung the noose for me
Just another form of slavery, clearly, I could see
In my case, Justice remained blind as can be.
Those people told everyone who could hear
that I was like a calculated cold murderer;
not fit to be among society, as if they were pure
Never mind the fact that I was the victim
in my own home when intruders tried getting in!
No one was injured, but I could have been
And . . . silence is all I heard from my 'friends'

My beloved Father kept me strong,
as I held my mindset right, every day & night
He brought me out of the bloody hell's pit
For all the doubters and my conspirators . . . I'm still here
The erroneous accusations from Evil's spawns
no longer cause my dreams
to turn into day and nightmares
Sweet peace enters my soul areas
and the essence of my life,
centers around our Master above;
He keeps me home in His incessant love

Showers of Blessings

Sometimes he remembers me
When he calls my name

Sometimes there's confusion about who is he
And delusion from who he used to be
My heart becomes happy
When he recognizes me

I love when he looks deeply into my eyes
Memories unforgettable of my robust patriarch
Glowing softness in his beautiful brown eyes
My soul smiles and dances . . .
Grandfather's favorite song

Showers of Blessings . . .
That's what I receive
When God blessed me with the opportunity
To love
To help
To assist
To serve
And to be there for him . . .
As needed

When father was murdered . . .
The only other loving male role-model . . .
Was this man
He showered me with love & blessings . . .

How great it feels to lend a hand
To the very man that fathered my mother
And nurtured me . . .
When I was a little girl
Grandfather was always
Loving
Caring
Strong
Helpful
And

Lana Joseph

Hella' hard working

Sometimes I wonder why some blood relations
Are waiting . . .
Idle . . .
Waiting for the end
I wonder why they pretend
Pretending to care . . .
Distancing themselves
Unwilling to help
Yet . . .
Focusing on the monetary
Proud to be an heir
I have no understanding . . .
On bended knees
I count my blessings
Blessed to enjoy the greatness of my grands . . .

Honored . . .
Humbled . . . as I lift my hands
Feeling their love
Filling my spirit
Giving all that I am
All that I can

Sometimes
I wonder
If it is enough . . .

I'm grateful for our time
Authentic
Sacred
Showers of Blessings . . .

*Dedicated to my beloved Grandfather, who had aged 94 when he transitioned. RIP, RWG & RIF (Rest in Freedom) with our Ancestors, my King Patriarch! I Will Love You 4Eternity Grandfather!

Beyond the Veil

I took off my veil
you made me feel the holy grail
you did not judge me
you inspired me
you uplift me constantly
you cleansed me with tears
you removed all fears
you embraced my weird . . . with love
I love your letters
I love your ink-spills
I love you, poetic souls
I love more than words_____.

Senses

EyE . . .
see your soul
smell your whispers
taste your mind
touch your cries
hear your Love . . .

The Matriarch

A **WOMAN** told tales of a hairbreadth escape
Out of the Deep South, with hundreds she fled
Poor **MOTHER**, breeding, and mated like apes,
Satisfying Master's sexual demands,
Sweet **DAUGHTER**, abused and dehumanized,
Sleep, tomorrow's harvest, crops, children borne,
LOVER on exhausted soil, fate realized,
Stolen youth, broken heart, a spirit torn;
A **WIFE** enslaved. She began to erode,
Seeds devoured . . . perpetrator's power,
Courageous **SISTER** broke defense's mold,
A long rest from wearing the tree every hour;
FRIEND, I'll enjoy life as no tomorrow
Your anointed home, no pain or sorrow

You Remind Me of Mama's Garden

I loved mama's breathtakingly beautiful garden.
It grew momentous on a hill.
Some folks laughed . . .
just couldn't believe it was real.

YOU remind me of Mama's garden . . .
lively, exotic, spontaneous, uninhibited, creative,
connected, fresh, brilliant, radiant & luminous;
like her luscious vegetables, herbs, spices,
flowers, fruit trees and sooo much more.

Oh,
how I adored hearing the chirping birds' singing,
while watching lady bugs, butterflies and
bumble bees dancing!

Mama designed a steadfast foundation,
while nurturing nature's roots & vines.
In this garden, I could always remain receptive . . .
as did everything around me.

Breathing awakening, intuitiveness, playfulness & joy,
while being liberated without any holding blocks.

YOU remind me of Mama's garden . . .
a beautiful piece of heaven here on earth.

YOU
ARE
ALL
precious gifts from GOD.

Summer, winter and fall . . .
happiness always filled feeling souls;
like flowing streams & rivers . . .
Mama's garden joyously took hold.

God's Radiance

Sowing good seeds . . .
presented profound powerful presents & presence;
these inspiring honored connections . . .
between
ALL
OF
YOU
and me.
Like Mama's beautiful garden . . .
YOU have illuminated & motivated me
and my world . . .
in ways that only YOU Artists can.
Humbly, I thank you!

You remind me of Mama's garden . . .

*This scribe is for YOU, my stellar artist family! Thank you, beloved Kings and Queens, for sharing your beautiful souls with me and for allowing me to be a part of your world. You have enriched my life more than I can express. You all remind me of Mama's beautiful garden. I Love You!

From Sunrise to Sunset

Awaken sunrise
The spirit of birth's grace flies

Nakedly I came
With no fortune or fame

Virtuous visions and unchained frailties
Knowing humbleness, I echoed no realities
Living in the lap of earth's obscurities confined
Blessed breaths blowing miracles on mankind
Misery in sincere-less foes,
Sleeping beneath damnation-holes

Despises those with blessed spirits
Who invest in paradise's treasure chest

Glowing dawn, day to day
Meeting others whose soul relate

Cherishing mute-less smiling eyes
Glaring at heaven's uncharted skies

Motionless and trembling in hope's mirth
Remembering my weeping humble birth

Throughout these soaring years in deep
Dreaming symphonies of gentle sleep

Fragments of fate's prophecies
Bridges crossed beneath sunless seas
Many times, dreading those left behind
Measured beyond un-honored dead fires

On earth, their courses wandered,
Smiling in scorn as lost liars

Sunset wings of kindred spirits rejoice
Birds singing noiseless songs unvoiced

God's Radiance

Shadows move to calm the night's invisibility
Leaving no room for gloom and misery

No hidden truths or a wayward strife
I stay in the bosom of God, my life

Lana Joseph

When You Awaken Tomorrow . . .

When you awaken tomorrow,
if you find that I'm no longer there with you on earth,
I know you're crying tears of loss for me . . .
and you're deeply feeling sorrow.
Please try to understand,
it was my time . . .
just as it was for my birth.
My life was truly blessed.
We did many wonderful things together . . .
and shared so much fun and happiness.
Just know . . .
our love is forever tethered.

Perhaps you're thinking of some things
that we did not have an opportunity to say or do.

Please know that it's okay.
I pray the tears you shed for me will soon lessen,
and you can feel how much I still love you.

I know you will always love me too.
That's the most wonderful blessing of all.

So, when you awaken tomorrow,
and I'm no longer there,
I need you to know this:
Our beloved Father above sent a beautiful Angel . . .
to bring me to heaven with Him.
I am truly grateful that God prepared a place for me . . .
to live for eternity.

No, I did not want to leave you.
Death took me by surprise too
When you think of me . . .
please remember how I laughed and lived life to the fullest;
continue doing the same for YOU.
Live and enjoy the life you've been given.

God's Radiance

Some days will be great and some will be pretty awful.
As you think of me today in mourning . . .
Let sunshine warm your tomorrow,
Remember how I cherished life . . .
and loved the Lord with all my soul.

As time goes by and you think of me,
have solace in knowing . . .
I have no sorrow.

I thought that I would be afraid to die,
and the thought of never being with you again brought a tear to my eyes.
But when I saw the beautiful light of love
our precious Lord welcomed me home . . .
as He sat on His glorious throne

Think of how happy I am reuniting with my beloved mother and father.
Also, I'm with other loved ones who had already transitioned to Heaven.
Think of how wonderful I feel . . .
I'm filled with an overwhelming sense of joy that I've never experienced before.
My divinely blessed home with God is everything that was promised . . .
and oh . . . so much more.

No . . .
I will not have another tomorrow with you on earth.
My time there is gone;
It's a short visit from the start.

When you awaken tomorrow and you think of me,
I need you to remember that I am in my true form now,
And I am always there in your heart.

You have brought so much love and joy to my soul.
I need you to always know . . .

I love you!

*Dedicated to my beloved dear Best Friends / Extended Family: Queen Sister Creole "Monique" Masala; Queen Sister Jewels; "EnuffMediocre" King; King Gene EbonyPoet Cole, aka "EP"; King Kevin Bigham, aka KB; Queen Sister Janet Perkins Caldwell; Queen Sister Luna "Moon" Golden, and all of my Brother Kings & Sister Queens who have transitioned. (RIF) Rest in Freedom, my dear King Brothers & Queen Sisters! Thank you for sharing your Love & Light with me and the world! I Will Always Love You All!

The Hand of Time

Wishing I could turn back the hand of time
                          the clock
                          father time

wishing that the losses were not so hurtful to leave behind

wishing that I lived in a world where every hu-man being was kind
and had Love and respect for all woman- and man-kind
even the animals . . .
God's wondrous creatures

well . . . truth speaks . . .
some treat four-legged creatures better than they do mankind
wishing I could fix all the broken spirits crying out each day . . .
crying out in pure agony

many are begging for a chance to just be heard

I'm willing to listen

                      no judgment . . .
                      no opinion . . .
                      no smirking . . .

I just want them to have an opportunity to be heard . . .

to speak out . . .

to speak on . . .

to speak loudly and clearly . . .

without interruption

                my brother / Kings

                my sister / Queens

I wish that I could let you know that I am here to listen

God's Radiance

I am here to serve . . .
I serve a forgiving God and I am here for you

I cannot change the past,
and when the pain tries to paralyze me
I pray to our Heavenly Master . . .
and not always on bended knees, shall I need to
He hears me

I want you to know though . . .
I am here for you
I Love you . . .
I am your opportunity

        I am present

           The Hand of Time . . .

Out of the Shadows

Illuminating many colors of light
Standing for all queen SisTars
Her radiance is beyond bright . . .
Out of the darkness,
Ebony Flow-essence arrived.
She came to speak to damaged souls,
Souls that had lost their lit-light.

With a soft-spoken voice, she said:
"Please see yourself through me.
I need you to understand, you will be vindicated!"

Ebony Flow-essence continued speaking softly,
Yet very clearly:
"Look beyond the outer frame of all untruths.
Look beyond all of the bigotry.
Look beyond all of the hostility,
and know that I stand for all beautiful queens today,
all beautiful queens before you,
and all gorgeous queens that shall rise after you.

You all represent Queen Mothers of this earth.

Continue to embrace all colors, sizes, shapes, races and cultures.
You are the pioneers for those that shall soon come.
Please stay out of the darkness, divine ones.
When you remain out of the shadows,
you allow your stunning light to illuminate;
you help other queens thrive throughout this world;
you help princesses while they are still little girls.

We all go through life's trials and tribulations.
Yet, when we embrace each other,
we create a heavenly oneness and a respectful bond.
This sacred bond is a bind that cannot be broken____."

My Homage to All Queens & Queen Mothers

Mother's Day is a special day . . . I hope and pray that you all had a great day! Please know that you, Queens, are all special to me. Mother or not . . . you rule as a Queen. This one is for YOU! I Love You!

Queen Cleopatra
Queen of Queens' ancient Egypt
great woman to rule____
Queen Cleopatra
born before Christ . . . sixty-nine
many stories told____
No one living knows
not all truths or myths . . . Egypt
ancient secrets . . . smile____
Cleopatra Queen
inspiration . . . strength . . . ruler
many Queen SisTars____
remind me of her
inward and outward beauty
truth . . . resilient_____
you love and protect
you are natural nature
your intellect reigns____
you are Queen Mother
your foundation is strong . . . faith
female . . . fine . . . fierce . . . friend____
you are regal . . . grand
golden female . . . bold . . . brave . . . Love
Platinum Queens . . . rule____

Lana Joseph

Blue Sliding Doors

Past pains leave ghost shadows, lingering to plague the strong.
Admitting that I could no longer be strong was not an option . . .
I had my share of feeding egos all day long.

At the head of the line, eager to welcome another vision . . .
there I was waiting to wear the crimson veil of another story.
Even then . . . I continued to give God the glory . . .

At what point does one stop spoon-feeding the dead?
I always believed that soul-busters only defeated on the willing . . . and I was not . . .
Can a soul ever grow tired of eating lies filled with lead?

What possible gain can one achieve by staining arteries with colorful dye?
Do they not realize that we too have seen the Matrix . . .
and choose to say NO to the Bull-'ish?
I've been through Blue Sliding Doors and I came through by truth's eye.

Those ghost shadows spilled blue black blood over me.
I chose clarity over strength . . . for I had been strong for way too long . . . no longer . . .
That's when I knelt down on bended knees, and cried out, "Master, please!"

I was slipping to that place between dead and undead . . . clarity is a good thing.
I broke through the blue . . . my veins bled red again.
No longer did I need to house the enemy in my blind bosom.

I needed no more dead caucuses trying to steal what does not belong to them.
My angelic sacred inner voice . . . god within . . . reminded me that I am His,
and He is Alpha and Omega . . . those who show disdain is not my beginning nor end . . .

because I chose Him . . . and the inner god-me . . . the war is already a Win;
because I chose to Exit the Blue Sliding Doors . . . I chose Victory.

I waved good-bye to my past . . . there's no need to look back;
there's no need to always be strong to survive when you have Him.

Why?
Because all I need to do is keep stating Facts and tell the truth!
And . . . so what? This is my life!

God's Radiance

Excuse those who cannot understand me . . .
because they are too busy brewing negativity.

Now, it's cool . . . because I'm through.
I said bye-bye to Blue Sliding Doors.

Lana Joseph

Nubian Queens

This one's for you!

Nubian Queen . . . I
speak . . . Fears unleashed . . . for Masses
unleashed Fear . . . I stand____.
standing strong . . . I must
faith replaced all fears . . . not tears
nation's renaissance____.

Beloved Prince

today is a sad day for me,
and for everyone in the world who loves you
all i want to do is shout
i want to scream
damn! damn! damn!
i want to ask why?
but all i can do is cry . . .
this poetess can barely write
today, i lost a best friend
the world lost a legend
thank you for all of the years
you have given yourself to us
"when doves cry" i look to the sky
i will continue to pray for peace
i will look to see you in purple rain
thank you for being with me through tears
thank you for giving me life on down-days
thank you for being my celebration of love
i just realized . . .
no matter how much i write
i can never thank you enough
ever since i heard of "Prince"
your name came with seXy, fine
azz, man, male or the symbol
formerly known as purple one
and . . . i can go on and on
but . . . there is and was . . . only one you
there will never be . . . another Prince
there will never be another you . . .
a humanitarian
a lover of truth
a lover of justice
a lover of music
a lover of love
a lover of revolutionizing earth
not the way you serenaded us
i always knew you were special from birth
i always knew you were a chosen one
i always knew you carried the sun

shine . . . and shine on
no shade . . . no shade on you ever
you were an authentic God-servant
i always knew you were an angel
today . . .
April twenty-first twenty-sweet siXteen
this aching pain inside will not ease
i do not wish to say goodbye
physically,
i know you are here through your legacy
you left behind a multitude of music
for that i am forever grateful
but . . . i know . . . i . . . i . . .
i want to behold you here on earth
i have loved you my entire life
it was your time to go . . .
i know . . . i . . . i . . .
i know you are home
you are where you started from
where your true form resides
when that time comes
i know we will meet up again
i will look for you . . .
with your beautiful wings
and a crowned King
on the other side
today,
i will not say . . .
good-bye_____.

*Rest in Peace & Rest in Freedom, Beloved King Prince Rogers Nelson
(7.6.1958 – 4.21.2016)

Ageing

i believe my beloved mother aged gracefully
as well as my Grandparents and Great-Grandparents,
and so forth . . . and so on . . .
the ageing process is such a beautiful natural gift
maturation comes in many forms, seasons and levels of love
often times . . . lessons learned by humans are belated
it is a culmination of individual and collective experiences
nevertheless . . .
seasoned adults are considered old, senile and outdated
i love the idea of one's golden years, wisdom and gray hairs
i have such a divine appreciation of ageing
my ancestors were honorable, brave and heroic
their legacies helped shape who I am today
and many older adults provided for loved ones
with crimson tears and sweat for pay

with gratitude and humility . . .
i am thankful for all expected and unexpected blessings
although life's journey undoubtedly touched pain,
heartache and headache along their journey
and mine . . .
it is all a part of a renaissance

i am eager to continue learning ways to refine
healing . . . and growing wiser flourishing new milestones
triumphantly, ageing tastes like ripened berries on a vine
seeking knowledge and wisdom from various sources
reading . . . researching . . . connecting with beautiful minds
spiritually feeding my heart from the beauty within souls

while never forgetting the internal and external beauty
and the challenges of my ancestors;
i aspire to keep my foundation deeply rooted . . .
while savoring and praising my universal life force
and following the wise patterns of my lineage

Lana Joseph

from alpha to omega . . .
when the pulchritudinous ascension of this ageing Queen transpires . . .
generational prosperity will befall upon my descendants
prayerfully . . .
my fierce love and parenting convictions will prevail
while i am ageing gracefully in mind and body . . .
also . . .
i hope to leave a legacy of Love
cherished by everyone who kissed my soul____.

*Dedicated to my beloved beautiful Mommy & Queen Matriarch, Delores W. Norris (1942-20017); my beloved beautiful Grandmother & Queen Matriarch, Marie Hall Wilson (1920-Present); my beloved beautiful Grandmother, Thelma Jones, (RIP); my beloved beautiful Great-Grandmother & Queen Matriarch, Gertrude Henderson Wilson (1889-1924); my beloved beautiful Great-Great Grandmother, Queen Matriarch Ida Rush Henderson (RIP); my beloved beautiful Great -Great -Great Grandmother, Queen Matriarch Vicey Rush (RIP).

A Child Rose

Hey Rose!
What you doin' here?
You're all alone stickin' out like a sore thumb . . .

I'm mesmerized by your beauty;
just wondering where you came from.

You're standin' kinda balanced, like a guard on duty.
My house isn't far from here, you wanna come?
Ohhh . . . My bad . . .

You're just a flower; standin' here like a diamond in the rough.
From a distance you looked weak, but now I see you're pretty tough.
It's weird how you sprung up in this bed of dirty cracked cement sand.
Nothing even lives here; not even ole Joe, the town's homeless man.

Rose, I wish you could look around and see what I see.
You're the only thing here that's beautiful to me.
I guess it's true when people say, "God works in mysterious ways."
Today, I gave my favorite new jacket to a boy I hardly know
But he was the only one at my school that treated me nice,
and would say, "Hey!" Or "Hello!"

I have no real friends at all; most kids just tease me.
All I have is a lot of problems going on with my family.
Until this moment Rose, I was thinkin' about takin' my life
Yeah, committing suicide seemed the only way out
I just wanted out! Out the problems, and out of family strife.

Then God led me to you, so strange . . .
Puff! Here you are standin' tall . . . right outta the blue.
Now my whole mentality is rearranged.

Even in the midst of a cracked and unclean foundation
The Lord has shown me your strength and beauty.
Thank you for helping me see my own situation.

You are me, Rose . . . and I am you.
Father God, thank You for sendin' Rose.
Thank you for showin' me . . .
I have inner strength,
and I can rise too.

*Based on a true story, this scribe is dedicated to a little boy who was not saved. The beautiful boy, who took his own life, hung himself later in the evening after giving my son his new favorite jacket. When my son arrived home with the jacket, I asked him about it, and he shared with me that it was a gift from a boy at school. Since my son did not have a phone number for the boy, I told him that I would go to his school the next morning to find the boy who had given him the jacket. Unfortunately, it was too late. This happened many years ago. However, I sat down and wrote this scribe, because I am still hearing stories like this one. Even though my son and I never really knew this boy, I have NEVER been able to get him out of my mind, my heart or my soul. Please recognize the signs. There are usually many of them. I am not professing to be an expert about this serious issue. I only wanted to share what is in my heart and soul. Children mean more to me than my words can ever express. I love them dearly, and my heart bleeds for them. I pray to God that all children are saved before they take their beautiful precious lives. Please know . . . this is one of the most difficult scribes that I have ever written. The words are simple, but the content leaves me beyond saddened.

The most current statistics I could obtain is from 2009. Suicide is the third highest cause of death among teenagers age 15-24. Suicide rates have doubled for children of 5-14 years old in the past generation. Teenage suicide is not caused by any one factor, but likely by a combination of them. Depression can play a massive role in teenage suicide. In 2007, suicide was the third leading cause of death for young people ages 15 to 24 – 1 of every 100,000 young people in each age group. Children, ages 10 to 14 – 0.9 per 100,000; adolescents, ages 15 to 19 – 6.9 per 100,000; young adults, ages 20 to 24 – 12.7 per 100,000. Nearly five times as many males as females, ages 15 to 19, died by suicide. Just under six times as many males as females, ages 20 to 24 died by suicide. [Sources: Wikipedia, the free encyclopedia, NIMH (National Mental Health), Suicide in the U.S.: Statistics and Prevention, research by James W. Prescott, Ph.D.]

Quietly . . .

Quietly through the storm
thunderously bent . . . lift lows
gasping thighs . . . shift highs
trying to find myself again
balancing curves . . .
unbalanced natural things
need to even the scale
need to bring me back
back to myself

Quietly . . .
through the storm
i find me again
still needing . . .
still wanting . . .
to balance the scale

Quietly . . .

Lana Joseph

Love Now!

sometimes there is none . . .
not enough time to make time
children grown and gone
yet . . . time sliiiiiiiiiid on by
twisted conceptions . . . touched pain
tasted defeat's wing
grace . . . mercy . . . prevail . . .
gifted quills . . . ground ourselves . . . truth
Savior . . . spills savor
past . . . present . . . future . . .
the faithful hand of time . . . love now
taste positive seeds_____.
Be encouraged . . .

Red Rain

He took me to a place
where I felt no more pain
and washed away misery
and red rain
With him I could no longer pretend
happiness
He's God-sent
He found me
and covered me with a cloth
I wanted to move,
but my body was sloth
He was amazing
smiling
gazing
holding me mysteriously in his eyes
tenderly
quietly
bathing me till sunrise
massaging my tears . . .
kissing red rain
My mind
my body
my heart and soul
transcended
spiritually, I followed
his footprints . . .
as he tended
and mended
broken heart-wounds
His foundation created an ease
Sweet Peace . . .
Now I can release
Love again___

Lana Joseph

Rise

majestic queens . . . still
rising sun . . . and suns . . . clean
transcending reason____
bathing smiles hidden
earthly fields . . . aroma-fed
saving souls succumb____
liquids tainted . . . blind
no explanation . . . sunrise
collaboration____
one by one . . . they come
beauty in all shades . . . Loving
children . . . we must save____

Immovable

I want to shout
cannot stand still
brothers and sisters
it is time to build
build a binding bond
become immovable
for our divine children
there is no time to chill
everywhere they are
be vigilant past dawn
do not give up hope
those with dense lenses
change mindsets within
we can change the world
help our sisters and brothers
poisoned by Flint's H20
our power is unimaginable
when we unite one love
children will follow suit
on earth and above
perfectly
we are created
our omniscient Heavenly Father
loves us as we are
beautiful shapes, sizes and colors
light and tar . . .

Irrelevant

My shadow cries on . . .
golden touch . . . isolation
I hear sounds of love_____.
And . . .
Before I depart earth
I do not wish to be irrelevant
I want to help change the world
I want to make positive differences world-wide
I want to help stop air, water and food pollution
Plaguing human being seems to be a theme . . .
I want to help stop faulty people from harming our youth
and seasoned adults, preying on their vulnerability
I want to help educate young and old alike
Removing historical untruths would be a great start
Enough with the diseased fables . . .
I want to help stop violence and bigotry of any kind,
Particularly domestic violence, police brutality & hatred against any group of people
I want to help young people have affordable higher education
I want to help create a world in which we, the people, could live in peace
I want to live in a universe where world peace is not just a dream
A dream that I still hold onto . . .
I do not want to transition from earth and end up being irrelevant!

God's Radiance

I Live Here

I live here for now . . .
Needing . . . no separation
Love . . . our creator_____.
Brush strokes flowing . . . souls . . .
Painted masterpieces . . . pure
Only one Savior_____.
Tasting Love's divine . . .
touching art . . . she rose within
Beauty everywhere_____.

Moment to Moment

Reaching out . . . arms stretched
thanking our creator . . . shine
earth whispers divine____.
I stand in silence . . .
listening to my inner-voice
hearing my Father speak in tongues I over-stand
joyously I stand tall . . .
no complaining at all
wondrously appreciating the beauty before me

Affirming His intentions with no distinctions . . .
between or betwixt races
You see this temple before you is sacredly divine
I love it . . . it's mine . . .
and
I give thanks to my Master for covering me with love's armor
my soul smiles with radiance
eyes may not see . . .
but can you feel beauty from soul to soul?

Will you stand with me for awhile
and look beyond this horizon?

Let's rejoice on earth with our honored temple.

Moment to moment cannot be contained,
just as one cannot place a shadow in a vial . . .

May I have this opportunity to shine with thee . . .
before our illuminating shells return to earth's dust?

No worries for tomorrow, dear hearts
for it will come for some . . .
today is our present-tense
our gift from the divine 1,
and for me it makes good sense

God's Radiance

I

L-O-V-E

and

R-E-P-E-N-T

Gratitude

ThankYouMyBelovedCreator4Life

Tears . . . pain . . . bleed within
praying . . . fighting . . . mercy . . . grace . . .
sane . . . insane . . . flip-flop
dragon slayer . . . not
He . . . relieves my ills immune
. . . system back to health
I kneel . . . gratitude
I knead . . . fortitude
Taste his love . . .
through You.

Black Pearls

Cold winds whoosh down on me under stars
while pieces of life are woven into a tapestry,
I move and am moved to adventures afar.

Mothers, Sisters and Aunts, "Born Free"
Born from one source we grow into disparate lives,
Dwindling time pushed forward by a stormy breeze.

What we have become supersedes binding ties
The tock of my heart slowing down in silence
We tread relationships which move current highs.

Remembering the forces of our movement unites
Preoccupations continue to obscure our sight
I embrace memories and old patterns to new heights.

The blackness has not changed Sisters' spurious slight
Aunts sweating, crashing, carrying sand for eyes
Mothers surrendered not to inertia; waterless tears die.

Mothers, Sisters, Aunts – veins of space and time
Phenomenally beautiful you are, what you leave behind.

I'm Tied . . .

I closed my eyes in thought of you
and tasted the withered sun-dried wind . . .
upon my face
reminiscing . . .
us kissing away pain-stained memories of yesterdays
today is all that is relevant
moment to moment with you in my mind
. . . and on my tongue . . .
I'm tied

A Dream, Realized

Taking hold of vision's beauty
Sacrificing true strength
Courageous actions made full
Streaming stillness silently sent
Fiercely wading in hopeful duty
Ringing desire's majestic deed
Divine journey, abandoned not
Spilled blood painfully bled
Reaching protection's pure lot
Floating hour's praying seed

Shadow & Death (No Masterpiece!)

     I see You . . .

   I see Me

I heard a resounding . . .
Pounding . . .
You're Found Guilty!
Ohhh . . .

NO!!!

WTF!!!

I sat SCREAMING inside!

Could not SHOUT OUT!

The judge shouted . . .

"Straight to Maximum Security"
"Criminal"
"Prisoner"
"Convict"
That's it!

Who?
ME???

At that very moment
I lost my identity
NO!!!
"That's not Me!!!"

My Father
My Master
My God
Please help me now!

With a closed fist

God's Radiance

Scattered . . . broken . . . lost
Locked down
In this tank, bleeding!
Brain . . . body . . . teeth freezing
Numb . . . feeling dumb-founded
Nothing!
That's Me!

Stripped down
Tied . . .
And bound
All orange
Shirt . . . pants . . . shoes . . .
Undergarments
Worn and torn
Too
Cast away . . .
Time
No longer mine
Muse . . .
Turned mute
Bled . . . then fled
Destroyed . . . Rep
Inmates' eyes
I cannot write
I don't wanna see
Mirror, mirror on the wall . . .
I cannot stand tall

No uniqueness
Inside . . .
U don't mean shit
To those staring Eyes
Cold
Cold
Icy Cold

Metal Mornings
Iron Days
Steel Nights
No Lights

Lana Joseph

Brains frozen
Lost
Tick-tock
No clock
Stretched within time
Release schedule
Dared . . .
And double dared
Who cares?
Time measured . . .
By Devil's lair

Finally, I saw
Behind ghost-whispers
Ravenous brains decaying
No longer works of art
No bars may they depart

Striking
Dazzling
Spectacular
Just a few literary adjectives
For this Muse
Now Me . . .
I . . .
And It . . .
Are dreadfully deceased

What happens to a Masterpiece
That sleeps with an Iron Phantom?

Doing time . . .
Trying to call my Muse
But can't get through
Putting lead to paper
Hoping
But Nothing
Still mute

I can only write what I hear
I can only write what I see
I can only write what I dare to dream

God's Radiance

And . . .

It's so damn N-O-I-S-Y!
Never quiet
Screaming
Yelling
Crying

I wanna SCREAM . . .
SHUT UP!
A-H-H-H-H-H-H-H!
PLEEEEEASE!
SHUT UP!

But the Bunkie 'cross from me does instead . . .
And the next morning that inmate was found dead
Another body, less to count
Added to the silent ghosts . . .
Laid up somewhere on a mount

Another fresh reminder
From the inmates in the tank
I'm not in control of me
I'm not in control of anything . . .
In here
Shortly before I came
Another inmate was found dead
That's what they said

That's what they told me . . .

Those sounds are becoming waaay too familiar now

Clanging
Clacking
Clinging
Banging
Bamming
Beating

A L W A Y S K E Y S

Lana Joseph

        E

        Y

        S

A L W A Y S

        K E Y S

Seems time slept silent
She's the only quietness seen

Voices are heard in the deep dark night
Madness appears in velvety light
Lunacy cannot be restrained
Keys will not open those deadbolt locks
Mindsets become metered like a wrist-watch
While souls are obstructed by Satan's vile-ness

Astonishing
Remarkable
Surprising
Amazing
Spectacular
Stunning

That used to be Me

Each and every day
I prayed to stay safe and sane
While trying to refrain
And keeping the enemy
From tainting my brain

And . . .
It is still YOU, Kings and Queens!
Please realize . . .
You are not like the others

God's Radiance

Many have given up!
They were career inmates
On the inside . . .
Many . . . many . . . many . . .
Minds are institutionalized
Crippled and immobilized
Many times before . . . times ten

But . . .
YOU . . .
My beloved dear hearts
Are made to win!
As you walk through the valley . . .
Of Shadow and Death . . .
Always remember . . .

YOU
Are
A
MASTERPIECE!

*To the women and men imprisoned by an unjust system in the society in which you live, please know that you are A Beautiful Masterpiece. God has given us all gifts. You are not alone. Our Heavenly Master is with you, and He loves us all. I hold you in my thoughts and prayers. To everyone that are affected and / or effected by the imprisonment of a loved one, please let them know, they are indeed a Beautiful Masterpiece; created perfectly perfect by our loving Creator. Thank you! (This poem is a revised version of my original scribe, "No Masterpiece!")

Love Without Wings

Through the tears that stained tattered hearts
we tasted varnished bitterness 'til it turned to dust
Wanting not to want what was not ours to claim
shifting perspectives made us see the power within
I
and We
Understood . . .

that happiness would come
Managing pain is a must
Joy replaced condolence's purple red rain
The sun rose again
The moon smiled upon cinnamon

We bathed in happiness
and embraced love without wings . . .

~ Ubuntu ~

All Blessings Are Good to Me

I was told . . .
"All blessings are not always good."

I said,
"That's your perception. Wow!
All blessings are good to me!"

Later, I made a list of synonyms for the word "blessing", and related these terms to my personal life.

BLESSING:

sanctification
absolution
benediction
commendation
consecration
dedication
divine
sanction
grace
invocation
thanks
thanksgiving
advantage
asset
bounty
break
favor
gain
gift
godsend
good
good fortune
good luck
help
kindness
lucky break
manna from heaven

Lana Joseph

miracle
profit
service
stroke of luck
windfall

Guess what?
Everything on my list
reflects the positive attributes
that I experience on a daily basis.

Even when negative things in my life happen,
I still feel the blessings that are bestowed upon me
when I love
when I read
when I write
when I smell
when I taste
when I see
when I hear
when I touch . . .
I know that I always want to be a blessing to others
My family and friends mean the world to me . . .
And . . . I am truly blessed with beautiful creative souls
that sprinkle showers of blessings upon me daily.

I feel as though I am "over-average blessed!"

*"over-average blessed" is a quote from my beloved Grandfather, King Patriarch, Howard D, Wilson Sr. I Will Always Love You Grandfather!

Chilled

        Decisions made
        Souls
        Must redeem

Hear spring's youthful call
Warm rains and night eyes play tricks
Cries, screams and applause

        Ocean tears
        Haunt
        Choices fade

See autumn leaves fall
Saying goodbye to lost loves
Shadows of decay

        Amber grave
        Darkness
        Stabbed pain

Touch winter sadness
Frosted death's cold poverty
Endlessly, I pray

        Ills fog
        Bones
        Death, slaved

Taste summer's blood moon
Boiling skies' passionate kiss
Silent heartbeats, joined

        Soul slayer
        Shattered
        Evil's door

Kissing tear-stained lips
Sunbeam rays boil ocean's floor
Mother sea calms me

Lana Joseph

       Christ Jesus
       Resurrect
       Dirt-born

Opening life's door
Souls torment and betray thee
Infatuation

              Gripping moments
              Redeemer
              Exploding reality

Smell fall's golden air
Leaves brown, yellow, orange and red
Life's splendor revealed

              Fallen fantasy

              Chilled

A Jazzy Good Time

The mood was in me
listening to Coltrane
tasting soul food in the rain

senses stirring moist
covering me with Davis, Miles
fingers tracing smiles

serenading wet
tasting Wilson's "Crazy Love"
imagination wild

ravenous duet
swishing baths . . . Otis Redding
climbing Ellington bed-posts

no more solo highs
no more lone George Benson-rides
play "Billie" . . . baby____.

A Love-Letter

Embrace me, my love
Hold me in your smiling soul
Please don't let me go

Let's not grow apart
This interlocking bound love
Is sent from above

Our bond is not sex
It's that spiritual lust-kind
A blessing to find

Captivating love-bliss
This is the real raw jones' thing
It's not often seen

Let me love you hard
We have been given God's gift
It's rare and priceless

Love can be scary
Sometimes it's overwhelming
God sanctioned this one
~ Ours ~

Rings

rings and heart-strings . . . smile
unconditionally . . . we
conditional . . . he

love left . . . loving me
bringing forth rings of love . . . lost
found . . . internally

soulful love is best
for me . . . He created . . . He
looks for love in thee____ .

Lana Joseph

God's Babes

When I see the innocence of a babe

smiling with the angels

I know within . . .

God isn't done with human-beings

Sins are forgiven

L-O-V-E____ .

U-N-I-T-Y

U-nity . . . love . . . light . . . harmony and peace

N-o i say to hatred & discrimination

I-lluminating beauty is in all God's creatures

T-ogether we can serve beyond transcreation

Y-ou, me and we . . . are all one dust of love

The Scribe in Me

piercing deeply into my skin . . .

i was set apart to take a fall

as the serpent used his avatar's fort

my Master's mercy erased the sin

while the enemy's attempt plagued nature's call

i bounced back the ball in evil's court

in which was scribed therein____.

Organic Love

welcome sunshine . . . day
beautiful life, breathtaking
giving thanks . . . most high____.

i freely serve thee
like-spirits are a blessing
thank you, beloveds ____.

you inspire me . . .
i am deeply humbled, loves
please accept my hugs____.

praying for you now . . .
may your journey taste sunrise
inner-child . . . peace . . . feel____.

The Innocent

Innocent children . . .
caress them gently . . . in love
can we trust . . . in us?

Can they trust . . . in us?
we believe what we perceive
the essence of love . . . void

Many do their best . . .
to serve and protect children
yet . . . some . . . do . . . not . . . care____ .

The Beauty of Nature

Nature's beauty stands at attention.
All of God's creatures serve a purpose;
there's wonderment in discovering what He has destined us to be.
Will we as humans reach our fullest potential?
Will we stay true in honoring our God-given call?

Will we seek to produce sweet good seeds?
Will we remain open-minded in order to learn and grow from all experiences?
Will we shine like the bumblebee, while pressing forward to achieve our destiny?
Will we give homage and respect to all of God's creatures?

As we move about each day, enjoying the beauty of nature,
will we remember that this too is one of His divine gifts?

Will we realize that we are His chosen beings here in the universe . . .
Before we transition beyond space and time?

Will we just be like nature . . .
while being humble here on earth?

Shine on!

Shine on, Queen of Queens . . .
You are a True Queen
A beautiful stunning Woman . . .
A classy loving Wife
A beloved patient Mother . . .
A helpful affectionate Relative . . .
A respectful fierce Friend
A fantastic strong-minded Leader
A positive role-model for young girls . . .
Shine on . . .
Queen of Queens
I feel so blessed to know you
My Black, African American, Hispanic, Caucasian & Asian SisTars
You hold all of these dynamic characteristics . . .
And too many more to list.

Today,
I would like to acknowledge you
For all of the wonderful things you do;
I commend you for standing strong
During all of the Bull-'ish you go through.
Shine on Queen of Queens . . .
Because of you . . .
This world is much more bearable
You always know what to say . . .
Mending broken hearts
Even when yours is torn

It's amazing how you motivate people
You inspire the masses
Everyday . . .
You put a smile on someone's face
Your name is a badge of honor . . .
All of my incredible SisTars . . .
I celebrate your selfless actions on earth
I thank our heavenly Father for your divine birth

God's Radiance

I Love and adore you!
Beautiful powerful Queen of Queens . . .
Please continue shining on.
Queen of Queens . . .
Thank you for your divine inspiration & love.
I Love You with All My Heart!

I / EyE Love Nature

and natural hairstyles
and babies' breath morning dews
and love's blissful kisses

I / EyE Love nature
and fresh rain
and clean air to breathe
and dancing in the dark

I / EyE Love nature
and caressing man's hand
and love that can over-stand
and giving in to them

I / EyE Love nature
and creatures of His earth
and serving His children
and counting my blessings

I / EyE Love nature
and hope to help save the world
and make my mark upon humanity
and love fiercely our boys and girls

I / EyE Love nature
and pray for destruction to halt
and stand alone for truth when needed
and choose to stay true for me and you

golden chocolate

loving spirits . . . reaching out
comfortable . . . skin _____ .

embracing beauty within
shades . . . colors . . . gifts . . .
and . . .
I and Eye Love fiercely

there is so much on earth to enjoy
there are so many good and kind . . .
hue-man beings
yet, many choose to ignore
their "being."

I and EyE paint things
soulful lenses taste beauty
represent dark child_____ .

I give homage to my creator.
I give homage to my ancestors.
I love to adorn myself . . .

golden chocolate
loving spirits . . . reaching out
comfortable . . . skin _____ .

Earth-Days

Mother Earth, hear our cries
nurturing us you have done from birth
like any beloved mother you deserve respect
i apologize for those that could care less
i will continue to do my best
to protect you, Mother Earth
i love you and i thank you
to be alive is truly a blessing
yet . . .

death and destruction are out of hand
you have been a caring and loving mother
you continue to water all things living
you continue to provide plenty for us all
you continue to nourish us
like the great mother you are
yet . . .

i cannot stop the people from ignoring
i cannot stop the demons from murdering
i cannot stop the enemy from destroying
the plants
the trees
the flowers
the oceans
the birds
the animals
the skies
the water
the food
the land
the men
the women
the children
yet . . .

the earth is steadily revolving . . .

self-love

i will continue to strive for justice

i will not sit on my azz and shut up

i will continue to love on Kings and Queens

that love me and the skin I am in

i will continue to keep my head held high

and remain proud of my sweet melanin

i will always love my divine god within

and the mahogany Queen

I am____.

Purple Love

there are times one must pause
all we have is love
cherished memories
soul-kissed
smiles . . .
and dimples dancing eyes

there are times when we witness geniuses
in our midst . . .

sometimes . . .
these earth angels are closer than we know
sometimes . . . we miss the opportunity to love
or to show love . . .
today, i want to reveal
from the depth of my soul
i love you all
my beautiful kings and queens
you phenomenal poets and poetesses____
I will always love you, phenomenal Prince!

*RIP, RWG & Rest in Freedom with our ancestors.

Here EyE Stand

I stand and gaze
upon faces and eyes filled with love
beatific . . .
handsome . . .
gentle faces
. . . empty spaces
a maze
amazing
such astonishing works of art . . .
within art
like You, my beloved Family
I gaze at You
and Your Beauty
Here . . . EyE stand . . .

Beauty is everywhere
EyE see Beauty in You
EyE Love You All!

Always 1 God, 1 Love

Loving life . . . nature . . .

Abundance . . . God gives freely

SisTars . . . Brothers . . . LOVE . . .

Enjoying life . . . full

Filled with Love; pain deleted . . .

1 God . . . 1 Fam . . . LOVE!

What If?

What if I told you that beyond my pulsating heart

lies your galvanized throne?

What if you took the time to hear my soul

to see exactly where is home?

What if illusions of happiness . . .

are not in the shadows of virtual realities' door?

What if you could feel synergy awakening

darkness

and releasing pain from heart's core?

Glory

Feel my flow this day

Humble, I hope I always stay

Love . . . Sisters . . . Brothers . . .

soulful love embraces all colors

I Love You!

Blessed to Connect

I am . . .

because you are He

that resides in me

Thank you . . .

I'm blessed to connect

with divine like-souls

What Makes My Life Sparkle . . .

. . . awakening from a dream on a winding expedition,
happy to hold my mother's smile in my eyes

. . . watching sunshine twinkles in the souls of children,
dancing with wings of golden fireflies

. . . laughing aloud with him who holds the key,
while playing with the little boy inside of him

. . . spending quality time with beautiful seasoned adults,
enjoying every moment of serving their needs and wants

What makes my life sparkle . . .

praying incessantly
Loving authenticity
meditating unobtrusively
writing validity
dancing spiritually

What makes my life sparkle . . .
. . . there is so much more
that makes my life sparkle

. . . to name everything
is like naming all scribes I have abandoned

. . . there is always more to add
meanwhile . . .
. . . I continue enjoying happiness
while serving 1 bona fide King
What makes my life sparkle . . .
every day I awaken
I am given . . .
tranche de vie
(a slice of life)

Uncensored Thoughts

i want to fly
i want to stop feeling like a caterpillar
i want to become a butterfly
i want to taste her freedom . . .
drifting here and there
everywhere
unfamiliar places
praying to find home
praying to stay focused on the roads taken

unfamiliar . . .
familiar places
not taking anything for granted
remembering all things we did to survive
sometimes the rainbow is not enuf'
sometimes it is best to face unpleasant situations
head on . . .
it is always best for me to keep divine faith
even when uncertainty slaps me in the face

i pray for the day that stability stands still
allowing me the opportunity to stop____.

i want to fly
i want to stop feeling like a caterpillar
i want to become a butterfly
i want to taste her freedom . . .

Will You Catch Me as I Fall?

As I fall, my smiles turn to screams
As I fall, my joys turn to sorrows
As I fall, sunshine turns to thunder showers

A hollow heart, heartbreak caused
Eternal hole, whole-hearted
Blood stained tears, tearing soul's morrow

Your unspoken words have spoken volumes
Your actions have shown what you truly mean
Your unseen and foreseen has guided mystery in what you see

Expeditiously, I had hoped you would see me
Urgency needed, I am diving deeply into abyss
Will you catch me as I fall?

Can I just be me for being me?
May I have an opportunity for you to see me?
Will you accept me, as me, and let that be?

Hurry . . .
Save this soul's lingering pain . . .
Will you catch me as I fall?

*Inspired by Mangus Khan's "As I Fall". My Beloved Dearest Friend, Mangus, thank you for being my Muse for this piece. I appreciate you and your continuous love and support. You are a brilliant writer. Keep on letting your quill flow. Much Love, Queen

Why I Write

because it is in me!
writing is my Love!

Yes . . .
I am in Love with words
I am in Love with Letters
I am in Love with Poetry . . .
. . . and short stories
. . . and play scripts
. . . and novels
. . . and essays
. . . and now Blogs

I write
because everything that embodies writing
awakens my true being
everything has beauty
I seek to find it through this gift
through my work of art
through my visual images
in the depth of my scribes . . .

you can touch me
you can taste me
you can feel me
you can hear me
you can see me
I kiss words
and taste many flavors . . .
on many occasions
I simply sit in silence to savor them
I am
blessed
I am
connected
I Love

like-minds
and beautiful
creative spirits . . .
I write because
it is like breathing fresh air
after a rain shower

I am comfortable
I am content
I am blessed
I am in Love

I Love Everything
I can imagine
in this Galaxy
and beyond

These are a few reasons . . .
why I write____.

Love and Happiness Is . . .

For me, my one and only love
It's about the love and happiness we share as one
Our blessed love is built on a foundation of divinity
God has united us,
And together we can continue to move positively
We have the most precious love of all
Unconditionally . . . selflessly . . .
Keeping trust and faith in our Master above
I know that the trials and tribulations we face
Will have no strong hold or debase
As we continue this wondrous journey called life
Our world is engaging in warfare and strife
You and I have set goals, we remain focused
We're not sucked in to society's evils within
What our souls behold has no end
I inhale love and happiness every heavenly day
While others try to break our bond that forever binds
What they fail to realize is our spirits have God's ties
Our hearts and souls will never forget this love shared
Exceptional love is one we have declared
In spite of negativity, we have individually endured
On our voyage to find true love, I now hold loves cure
I've crossed paths of those whose only goal was to receive,
But since God brought us together,
True love is achieved
Your actions and authentic nature,
Has shown that you just wanted to know me
You've brought such passion and bliss to my world
I finally feel those words that I've often heard
Exhilaration, pleasure, delight, and ecstasy . . .
I now hold these feelings,
Because God brought you to me

My love
                         My baby
                         My heart
                         My friend
                         My man
                         My King
                         My Husband
When I speak of love and happiness
                         My soul smiles
                         My heart flutters
                         My palms sweat
                         My body tingles
                         My mind sings
                         My eyes dance
It's because of you
These emotions I feel are true
God made you for me
I know that I know
I'll be with you till eternity
My beloved King,
We were destined to be
You are the epitome of love's authenticity
I know I am blessed,
As I stand before you, I must confess
You are my true love and happiness . . .
My One and Only

Macroscopic Thoughts

Needing to speak through silence
hearing whispered cries in the background

Scattered words lie dormant in closed minds
rambling in space, wanting out and finding a way

Inspired by worldly experiences, subconsciously,
consciously motivated by things seen and heard

Confused by utterances muttered through masses
needing to write on chilled blank canvases

Soulfully painting images deeply felt
and speaking clearly words that melt

Do we hear one thing,
then scribe another?

Do we consciously,
unconsciously write for others?
As I sit in darkness, I often wonder
is my voice sonorously heard?

Personally,
I write for me,
and for the heir of my soul

But, do we have a responsibility
to be responsible with our words?

Our youth will emulate, what we say and do

When writing for a public cause, I will admit
I must choose my words carefully before I submit

Lana Joseph

No matter what I write, poetry or prose,
I can only hope that the interpreter knows

We may not see eye to eye on everything.
My twisted mirror shows life's transparency.

If negative criticism and judgment were replaced
with human emotions, null and void of hate;
then empathy isn't necessary to show kindness.
We can honor where a spirit is coming from.

I hunger and thirst for that divine day
when all ink pushers, respect . . . ability to say
written or spoken words for the masses,
simultaneously presenting, works everlasting
Maintaining decorum and respect for this gift
is having free discourse and keen awareness

Expressions shared from one to another,
sacred souls succumb under our umbrella

Please understand, as grown folks,
I'm not referring to 'adult content'
Humbly I pray, we are in agreement,
children are holding our words too

I'm just sayin'
my
macroscopic thoughts

Looking out the Window . . . Waiting

Looking out of the window . . . waiting . . .
Waiting . . .
hoping
praying that these tears i shed will someday bring me comfort
cleansing
dripping red rain-stained glory befell
my lips chapped
my mouth parched from the screams
the cries of change yet to come
crying out the past shadowy remnants

Doing my best to stand tall . . .
wronged
battered
whipped
slashed
someone called my name from beyond the grave
shouted and screamed
saving me
to enslave me
brutally brutalized me
i feel as though
i died in the Killing Fields.
Why?

This entire structural foundation is going astray
many men & fathers are brutalizing their women and children
many women & mothers are acting like party girls gone wild
many children are strangled by the tentacles of their parents
watching & emulating their behavior . . .
while parents tell their children
"do as i say, not what i do"
Who's the fool?

Lana Joseph

Many excuses continue
fingers pointing daily
but the twisted roots tell the truth

When all is said and done
do we blame the architect?
Or do we blame the architecture?

When i turn on the news
i see many more youth
dead.
Yes . . .
i wait
i weep
i fear
i grieve
while i'm looking out of this window pane
i yearn to rejoice . . .

As time goes by some things change
and some remain the same
lives are still being lost
men and women are still falling prey
to evils inwardly & outwardly everyday
racism does still exist
even though some wear sheets
underneath . . .

Hatred is diseased
it's cancerous

Many are judging
mistreating
killing
lying & stealing
from those who barely have enough to maintain
and there are others that sit on their high horse

God's Radiance

pointing fingers
looking down on people
treating them worse than children of the corn

When all they need is
Unconditional . . .
L-O-V-E

Just like you and me
positive change will come
when everyone of us can look in the mirror
and recognize the truth
we are all the same
bleeding red rain . . .

*Inspired by my beloved Brother King Addonis Parker

Shining Beyond the Blues

desire to win
marketing stepped up their game
Queens reign industries . . .
bold and fierce truths told
chosen few . . . cloaked golden rain
royal . . . diamonds

no clan shadows stare . . .
on auctioneer's block . . . beauty
she slays . . . rising sun

always set a queen
upon her throne . . . where He . . . King
will present Love's flow
his path leads to her
hold on queens . . . due time
embrace light dark wings

Dear Lord gave choices . . .
breathe faith . . . pray for King's sacred life
birth to transition

sometimes there is none . . .
not enough time to make time
children grown . . . and gone
yet . . . time sliiiiiiiiiid on by
twisted conceptions . . . touched pain
tasted defeat's wing

grace . . . mercy . . . prevail . . .
gifted quills . . . ground ourselves . . . truth
Savior . . . spills savor____.

past . . . present . . . future . . .
faithful hand of time . . . love now
taste positive seeds_____.
Be encouraged . . .

Will You Unmask You?

Unmasking . . . my soul
I have done my best . . . I stayed
They showed no caring

Yet, pretended need
And asked for my assistance
Came long distance

They said family . . .
Things were getting very rough
With an S on chest

I came . . . days were tough . . .
My help was a labor of love
No compensation

Their plan was unknown
I came to serve my loved one
They did not know me . . .

They said family . . .
Was in need . . . I was the help
I knew my purpose

I was a servant
They marveled at my worn smock
I took pride in it

My mask behind it
I wore as an honor badge
They did not know me . . .
No time to unmask
My true purpose . . . only God
They said family . . .

With smiling faces
Holding lies . . . and smiling eyes
The S on my chest

Lana Joseph

Began to fade . . . light
His health began to fade too
And so did mine . . . blues

They called family
Replacements . . . distant kin-folk
They planned to remove . . .

One showed up to use
My smock fit the new family . . .
My loved one . . . removed . . .

He is now with God
He knows those who lethal dosed him
Those dark masks they wore
I released my mask . . .
Mask of protector of him
To this day . . . they did

I served my loved ones

My purpose fulfilled
Just like the Sun . . . perfect time
I removed the mask

And began to heal . . .
Many wear masks to guard souls
Our spiritual strength . . .
Helps us to unmask . . .
Time to face . . . and un-face off
Will you unmask you____?

Black Roses

Baby Sun . . . life's eternal
savior . . . Kings and Queens
knowing that you are marked before birth sets our sons . . .
apart from others . . .
like cattle raised up and sheep skins too pale to notice bellowing screams . . .
kissing tears stained crimson . . .
silencing madness and dark shadows tossed like roasting baby white marshmallows
and black roses . . .

Knowing that you are marked before earth welcomes you safely home . . .
from the womb we introduced ourselves and have loved you . . .
as injured souls yearning to breathe fresh oxygen
smothering decisions suffering bittersweetly . . .
we want you to live without fear in a world with no racism . . . no white supremacist . . .
    no brutality . . . no injustices . . . no lies . . . no sadness . . .

i want . . .

i want to taste the sunrise in mornings' dew

i want to use fingertip vibes caressing you

i want to feel raindrops captivating eyes

i want to fluff pillows tossed in the night

i want to hold dreams' doors 'til you arrive

i want to whisper love's unforgettable scribes

i want to fulfill God's plan for me with you

i want to add your last name an eternal bind

i want to always honor love's platinum badge . . .

Togetherness

Beautiful wings . . .

shades and colors

human beings . . .

sisters and brothers

come together . . .

Can we love one another?

I Love You!

I'm In Love

I'm in love
There is only one
A divine being
I went from blind to seeing

I'm in love
I desire no other
I live for Him
No longer aspiring to them

I'm in love
Love took hold of me
No need for desperation
I have the revelation
I'm in love
I want nothing, my needs are fulfilled
I can always trust and rely on Him
My soul is purely soothed from within

I'm in love
My spirit clings to Him
Our connection cannot be broken
He thinks my thoughts before they're spoken

I'm in love
And no one comes before Him
He owns my life, that is no lie
My need for Him, I will never deny

I'm in love
He's the greatest protector ever
And my continuous shining lit-light
Who always makes everything right

God's Radiance

I'm in love
He's my forever love,
Lord Jesus Christ,
Yeshua, Yahweh . . .
God created one
Holy Ghost, Father and Son

I'm In Love
It is He, that is greater in me
My Master of this world and above
It is He, with whom I am in love

I Will Never Forget!

The beauty of you and your divine spirit
live on inside of me . . .
although,
your physical transition still rains my soul with tears,
I will never forget you!
We were close in heart . . .
and a bit farther apart in years.
However, our bond was secure;
connected by our Creator.
We shared love beyond this galaxy.
You were my extended family:
a positive mother role-model,
true fierce friend,
an inspiring mentor,
loyal supporter,
and soooo much more . . .
You trusted me to direct your pride and joy
Your play,
The Bond That Binds,
Your beautiful smile lit up the theater during all performance nights.
I remember your mesmerizing eyes
glistening with pride.
Finally,
your dream was realized!
I helped bring your awe-inspiring play from the page to the stage!
The Bond That Binds made a huge impact for many communities,
our actors and actresses; including everyone involved with our production.
In my reflections,
I did not face your illness very well.
I believed that you would beat that horrible cancer.
You were a warrior Queen!
When you succumbed to that wicked illness,
my heart was broken!
The physical loss was too unbearable!
Your loving, kind, tenacious and vivacious spirit
touched souls in ways I could never truly explain.

God's Radiance

It has been said, "time heals all wounds..."
No longer am I certain about that statement!
It has been 11 years and 9 months since my beloved beautiful mother's transition from earth...
That wound never healed!
Yet, I am getting through it...
by our Creator's grace and mercy.

My beloved Mama Frances J. Betterson,
I will never forget all of the great times we shared.
I will never forget how blessed I am today,
because you existed in my life.
All of the fabulous memories of us together...
We faced the good, the bad and the ugly head on,
Never wavering in our friendship and love for each other.
That real raw "ride or die" kind of love and respect...
I will cherish those special moments
while holding you in my heart and soul for eternity.
I love you and miss you more than words & letters!
Thank you for all of the years that you and I were bonded!
Continue to RIP, RWG & Rest in Freedom with our ancestors.
Until we meet again,
my beloved beautiful Queen Mama Frances...

The Ebony King

Hello . . .

King?

Hey . . .

It's Me . . .
Queen

Do you mind?

May I have a few moments of your time?

Yes?
Okay . . .

Thank you . . .

You, beautiful strong black man
I'm here to give a shout out
And a tribute . . .
Because I can

To all my splendid Black brothas . . .

I wanna begin this conversation
By sayin'
I love you!
And God knows I surely do . . .

I mean no harm to you men of other shades
It's just that I love my brothas
From all those stunnin' black mothers
Or they've spawn from a line of noble black fathers

Do you hear what I'm sayin'?
I'm here to give them . . .
All black men
Unconditional

God's Radiance

Queen-love
After all the shhh you go through
Oppression tryin' to keep you down
Some would like nothin' better
But to see you wearin' a frown

You make me proud to be a black sistah
I'll never stop lovin' on you
Or being your favorite supportive girl
There's a lotta different men in this world
But I prefer my brilliant black brotha

Keep on keeping on . . .
Baby, just stay strong

I'm down for you and I got your back
Even when things go wrong
Hang on in there cuz'
You got it goin' on
Day after day
You get up and go to work
If you don't have a job
Some make you feel like a jerk
Please dear heart, don't worry
Just keep on standing tall
This Queen-love is forever
Forget all that bull 'ish
Don't let fools tug your balls

I appreciate your quality
You're a fine black man
I positively adore you

It's preposterous what you deal with
Somebody's dissing you all the time
But you still come out lookin' hella fine

Baby, they're just freakin' mad
Cuz' black men are inherently strong
It's true, you got it goin' on
While they're sittin' back hatin'

Lana Joseph

You won't be no puppet,
With your beautiful genius mind

Hold up . . .
Did you forget?

You're built better than a Greek god
Like Jesus Christ, a carpenter
You come from a royal star

You're great with your hands too
As in everything you do

I just wanna give you praise
For your incredible accomplishments
Sprung from hard work everyday

My intelligent radiant black man
You're exceptional
Gifted
Dazzling
Talented
You're skillful . . .
In all you do
Many have your college degree
You also gotta PhD
In common sense
While some folks have all the education
But know nothing about vocation
Those haters not worth two cents

Always remember . . .

Black is beautiful
Powerful
Courageous
Honorable
Lovable

Black Kings of mine
Don't break your bond
Just bind

God's Radiance

Listen up my brothas
My handsome black men
I'll always stand by your side

I honor you
I cherish you
And . . .
I choose you for eternity

Cuz' your spirited black Queen
Is incessantly proud of You

To tell the truth . . .
I don't need no ring
Just give me my Black King!

*I love you, Ebony Kings! Dedicated to my King, my Sons, my Brothers & all beautiful soulful black men

Angels in Unusual Places

No blood ties
Some never see them
Faces in the crowd
Some passers-by see her or him
Then they turn blind eyes

Nor did they see her pregnant belly
As she reached in garbage cans . . .
Looking to feed her unborn is necessary
Sifting through what others discard as trash
How many more will simply pass by
And ignore?

Not this bard!

Often times,
The creator will give a sign
All assets are not polished
Cleanliness is not always worn outwardly
i said, "hello"

Her eyes smiled behind the smudges
She looked up,
Sort of frightened
And then she mumbled, "hi"

i wanted to ask,
Can i help?
Can i get her some food to eat?
i did not want to embarrass her though . . .

i watched as her soiled hands
Ravenously rummaged through grimy fragments
Of bits and pieces of food
That were lying in the trash

i went inside the store
And bought a deli sandwich for her and her unborn

God's Radiance

When i went back to the trash can,
The perplexed woman was gone

i felt horrible and unsatisfied
i knew that she was famished

i only wanted to assist her

As i walked to the street,
i saw the woman rushing away carrying a sack
i called out to her
She turned and stared at me
With a puzzling look on her face
i could see her full face for the first time
She was stunningly beautiful
Behind the dirt and smudges
i saw the quintessence of her exquisite spirit

i crossed over to her
And handed her the deli bag

She gazed into my eyes
Reached out her hand to accept my offering
i wrapped my arms around her and hugged her gently
Not wanting to upset her or her unborn baby

A tear began to run down her face
i gazed back into her eyes
i held her hand and led her to a nearby bench
We sat there in silence
i watched as she ravenously ate the deli sandwich
i said nothing
Nothing was said
We sat
She ate
i saw God in her lovely eyes
i said nothing____.

Raven's Love-Letter

Ferociously, I fasted
Subjugated-ly, I released
Blissfully, I am saddened
Reverently, I am disrespected
Comfortably, I am discomforted

Empathy felt from soul's blood
Shed by lead from inhumane spirits
As bullets blast
Decades of discourse regarding human life
Such saddened souls shooting sifted shells
Ammo targeted for those melanoid kings, princes, queens and princesses

Those malicious ones continue to lash out like kneading tasteless dough
Choosing to have no regard for human lives
Leaving ebony bodies concrete cold
Lying numb
Loaded with accelerated slugs
And jubilant corpses lie like skeleton frames displayed for Halloween spectators

Empathy felt from ancestry souls slayed
By antagonist expeditiously discharging artillery
As I peer out into the world from my view
All I can do is pray for those transitioned divine souls
Their families and friends too
Also, I pray for all of us
I yearn for the day when human beings will unite
Under our Creator
One Nation under God . . .
For Liberty and Justice for ALL

Truth Speaks . . .
Judgment Day will come for everyone
The Corrupt will have their day for sure

God's Radiance

Until then . . .
How many more young and old black men and women must perish
By those who dwell behind the veil of righteousness?

Ferociously, I fasted
Subjugated-ly, I released
Blissfully, I am saddened
Reverently, I am disrespected
Comfortably, I am discomforted

*You are beautiful Kings, Queens, Princes and Princesses; spread your wings and fly . . . morning, day and night; stand victoriously in His bold light. I Love You Everyone! Please stay safe!

A Double Rainbow

Today,
i saw a double rainbow.

You remind me of her,
part of you in the spirit world;
the other still here on earth.
Transitions are not always swift.
Only God knows, the hours shift.

His son-shines, upon us all.
His son-shines, in spite of us all.
His son-shines, in us all.
Many have chosen dark over light,
Long before the fall.

Today,
i saw a double rainbow.

She reminds me of all hue-mans.
She reminds me of rain red.
She reminds me of His blood-shed.
i am drawn to the ocean calls.
A spiritual connection is in me.
It is where i love to commune.
Oceans sound like a womb.
i feel close to my mother.
i love visiting the ocean.
i can still hear God____.

Let Go!

Past pain
and poisonous words of disdain
no longer plague me.
I survived the hellish treatment
of evil trying to claim my soul.

      I was awakened with new purpose,
      and the opportunity to learn to let go.

      Holding on . . .
      was my way of keeping hope;
      but my eyes were shut
      and my mind was closed.

          I tasted the shattered fairytale
          that kept my life bound and choked;
          while evil's disguise drew blood,
          sonorously unprovoked.

          Then, my chalice overflowed.
          Clarity brought me out of despair,
          and into the shadows of light.

      Because of God's grace and mercy,
      the whispering winds of His energy
      gave breaths of love for life's flight.
      No longer did I carry a broken spirit.
      No longer did I bleed fear.

      He held my heart in His hands
      and removed my invisible shield.

Lana Joseph

As my eyes were opening again,
everything became crystal clear;
the essence of my soul was His.

      And . . .
      finally,
      I . . .
      let go!

Your Strength Lies Within

The strength of a woman
isn't seen in her face or her cheeks.
It's seen in the length of her arms
that embraces you within her reach.

The strength of a woman
isn't in the high tones of her voice.
It's in her soft sweet loving undertones,
which gives your soul a hoist.

The strength of a woman
isn't in all of the words she speaks.
It's in all the wonderful ways,
her word she keeps.

The strength of a woman
isn't in all of the friends she has.
It's how great of a friend she is to others,
and the children she comes in contact.

The strength of a woman
isn't how much she's admired and respected at work.
It's in how much she's admired and respected at home.
She loves and nurtures, even when treated like a jerk.

The strength of a woman
isn't how tough she can be when she needs to discipline.
It's how gentle and disciplined she is
by the love she gives and has within.

The strength of a woman
isn't in the physical beauty of her flesh.
It's in her beautiful loving heart . . .
that lies within her chest.

The strength of a woman
isn't in how many men she's ever loved.
It's in whether she can be true and faithful
to the ONE man she's trying to love.

Lana Joseph

The strength of a woman
isn't in the large objects or weights she can lift.
It's in the burdens of others, including hers
that she's able to carry, and some, makeshift.

The strength of a woman
isn't in how many people she loves.
It's in the understanding that the love she gives others
is purely unconditional.

A strong woman puts God first,
family second,
her work third.

My beautiful strong sisters,
your strength lies within your exquisite sweet spirit.

You shed those tears, as you're full of fears.
Just know that God hears.

Keep your faith in Him
when the impossible seems unattainable
and you're hanging in the balance.
Keep holding on and praising God.
Stay in your spiritual trance.

I love you and honor you,
beautiful strong women.

---

*Dedicated to my beloved beautiful strong mother, Warrior Queen Delores W. Norris (aka Queen Lady Dee): RIP MOMMY. I will love you forever; my beloved beautiful Queen Matriarch, great great great-grandmother Vica (aka Vicey); my beloved Queen Matriarch's great-grandmother, Minnie Lee Gipson-Hall, Gertrude Henderson-Wilson; my bonus great-grandmother, Syrentha Wilson; my grandmother, Marie Hall-Wilson; my beloved grandmother, Thelma Jones; my bonus grandmother, Annie Mae Norris; my beloved godmother, Queen Lesibee Wilson-Miniard; my beloved beautiful BFF & bonus godmother, Queen Mama Frances J. Betterson, and all strong Queen Matriarchs: May they all continue to RIP & RWG in Freedom with my ancestors. Additionally, this scribe is dedicated to my beloved beautiful Queen Matriarch, Rosemary Williams Smith. You have been a brightly lit light in my life, and I thank our beloved Creator Father God for choosing you to be my Bonus Mommy. I love & adore you beyond words & letters. Thank you for just being the awe-inspiring you . . . with me! And . . . thank you for birthing my King! Finally, I dedicate this scribe to all of my beloved beautiful Queen Sisters and all Warrior Women / Queens. I Love You All!

If Only . . .

I watched as you cracked opened pistachio nuts.
You enjoyed them as much as I did cashews.
Mmmm . . . those were indeed my favorite.

I adored hearing your voice.
You would appease me and read aloud
like I was a child.
Your bedtime stories always made me smile.

I loved the way you put your own spin on those old tales.
You were always so generous with me.
You gave all of your spare time to me . . . freely
I wonder if you think of me now?
I wonder if you remember my touch?
Do you remember my taste?
Did you forget my smell?

I wonder if you visit some of our secret places?
I wonder if you see me in your dreams?

I remember how you would tell me
that you would love me eternally.
Your beautiful brown eyes
were always watching me;
watching everything I did . . . daily.

I remember how special
and romantic that day was.
Your eyes were fixated on me.
I would use my peripheral to see.

I remember you lovingly
gazing deeply into my eyes,
knowing . . . I wanted you,
yearning . . . to be with you.

With every brush stroke,
I felt the gentle roughness
of your tender touch,

and then . . .
I felt earth's silence;
I heard rain in the forest.
You gave me all . . .
You.

I did not know there would be no we.

If I did . . .
I would have done more.
I would have paid attention more.
I would have shown you more.
I would have laughed with you more.
I would have prayed with you more.
I would have left you my legacy
and . . .
I would have loved you more.
I still do
If only____.

Strength & Determination

Once upon a time,
freedom was not an illusion.
This tribe, like many others . . .
naturally flourished.
Families were not suffering famine.
They were highly well-nourished.
People were not just tolerable inclusions.
Land . . .
Nature . . .
Animals . . .
Water . . .
Oils . . .
Gold . . .
Diamonds . . .
Like seasoned adults . . . were as precious
. . . as rare gemstones.
There were no comparisons . . .
. . . elders were loved and adored . . .
ancestors were revered . . .

Queens . . . nurtured their roles
Plenty . . . like Alaskan ice
Omo people smiled____.

Townships thrived . . . not died.
Authentic heritage . . . stayed.
Did they give good seeds?

Were they feeding tribes?
Will men hide behind the shade?
Queens exchanged . . . at what cost?

Omo couture . . . truth,
strength and determination
preserve their nature____.

Lana Joseph

Southern Africa . . .
there is a rampant beehive.
Contradictions . . . lie____.
Freedom was not an illusion.

This tribe . . . like many others,
naturally . . . freedom rang
until they came . . . for free____.

To Live a Life Full of PEACE and JOY

One must have an understanding
That everything we seek in life to be happy, we already behold,
While we are looking for happiness elsewhere
and finding ourselves caught up in a world full of strife.
If we would stop for a moment and breathe in silence to inhale the beauty of your soul
That is where we LEARN to love and have APPRECIATION for ourselves and others.
We were BORN with one spirit, and that same spirit is with us when we DIE.

I give THANKS and PRAISE to our heavenly Master
For allowing us the opportunity to love and LIVE.
Though DEATH is inevitable for every human being in his or her TIME,
God gave us GRACE so we could LIVE in PEACE and HARMONY in His Kingdom.
There we will be totally SAFE, and will forever ARISE, surrounded by BEAUTY;
While the Angels sing a FLUID MELODY of love everlasting.

On this day, and every day that we awaken here on earth,
We have been given an opportunity for spiritual RENEWAL.
Changes are bound to happen in one's life, but our spirit remains the same.
Loving our true self is a key factor to our happiness in the life we LIVE.
Imagine everyone one we love coming TOGETHER and spending quality TIME,
And everyone showing up with a high level of love for their true selves;
Additionally, each loved one viewing others as a vessel of love and light.
How powerful of a gathering would that be? Wow!

I do believe that we would have much more inner PEACE and JOY,
Which would spill over in our personal lives as well.
Certainly, there will be days that unpleasant things happen.
But I do believe through silence, prayer, and self-love,
One can overcome anything that life deals them.
In the end, no matter what is said or done,
Our true happiness ultimately lies within.

In Silence

Sitting in silence as the judge dismisses the case
inconsistent testimony
that was the reason used to set a murderer free

Why?

Because it wasn't his loved one . . .
that lost their life at the hands of a man with a knife

Simply . . .
"Case Dismissed".
All because the murderer's friends and family
changed their story in court under oath.

Yes . . .
they lied;
they lied to protect him,
the man who murdered my father.

So, there I sat silently . . .
stunned!
No Justice!
For me and my family,
justice remained blind.

My Soulmate

I thank God above
for my one & only true love.
He's my Man / King / Husband.
He's my Life-line & Soul-Mate.
He brought no negative drama.
His nature is natural as a dove.
He's incessantly patient and kind.
His wet juicy kisses keep me tight.
He respects the beauty of my mind.
He's adoringly honorable and real.
He's down right unpretentious.
His tender caresses, I love to feel.
He's never really overly anxious
He's what I call the real deal.
He's humble and down-to-earth.
His love and adoration are effortless.
He makes our love a beautiful rebirth.
He's sexy, strong, yet sincerely modest.
He works to keep our life trouble-free.
He's gently strong with smooth loins glossy.
He proudly exclaims his mad love for me.
He's everything I've dreamed & not bossy.
He gives me sweet romantic king kisses.
He's uninhibited and a pro with lovemaking.
He nurtures my feelings, never dismisses.
He's a wise man who's always reassuring.
He prays with me & for our dream wishes.
He's my one and only one divine King

(GOD SANCTIONED OUR UNION)

It's such a wondrous blessing
to have the man of my dreams.

He's so much more to love & adore.
He's a creator of artistic things.

He always views life more positively.
He's my natural true sacred King.
He puts God first and then me.
He's the only love for this Queen.
He makes my heart and soul smile.
He's my sexy, fine, adoring husband.
He loves and caresses my entire being.
His spiritual values match mine so tight.
He's philosophical with a brilliant mind.
His sexy voice woos & soothes me just right.
He's the man God made for me to find.
His love & adoration for me are spiritually real.
He's perfectly imperfect & perfect for me.
His authenticity, I continue to feel each day.
His name is written all over my anatomy.
He makes me feel we're on top of the world.
He's hard-working, and I admire all he does.
He works incessantly to take care of biz'.
His creative spirit always blends with mine.
He has shouted clearly that I'm his world.
He's everything to me because I'm his girl.
He's my Mr. and I'm his Mrs. for infinity.
He and I will transcend as husband & wife.
He works to maintain our blessed happy life.
He's the only man that I love and adore.
He is my divine love, sent from God above.

*Dedicated to my O.A.O.1 husband, King Rodney Dion Smith. Thank you for keeping our love and life an incessant adventure. Let's continue our journey together living, loving and laughing real hard.

The Climate Change

I am ready to travel
a reversal road.
I want to move on.
Children playing . . .
adults care . . .
I yearn for a hood.

Neighbors loving
smiles stare . . .
Community like I grew up in
true friends
and nosy adults.
Miss Walker and them,
always minding others' biz'
that was their jobs.
Being home on time
before the streetlights came on
that was my household's norm.

My siblings and I
and childhood friends knew the rules.
All of the rest
misbehaved in school.
Our parents and theirs would know
before we came home.
Nosy neighbors sucked!
They were a pain in the butt
to us children.

Not just my neighbor
next door to us or on my street,
or around the corners
in our neighborhood . . .
Our little community
around all corners,
from homes and each street
of my hood.
That's just how things were.

Lana Joseph

When I look back, I smile.
I have experienced
a drastic climate change!
The world I grew up in and
the communities I lived in
since my adulthood
have brought new perspectives.
As a child,
what I perceived as being nosy
were just concerned neighbors
looking out for one another.
Our parents and elders loved us
and protected us from harm.
People truly cared.
I want this hood back.
I want those nosy neighbors.
A huge "thank you" to them all!

I am in the process of relocating . . .
somewhere.
I am definitely ready for a change;
it is necessary.
I am holding on
during this reconstruction,
weathering the storm
of this climate change.
I hope for the best.
My midnight's
turning into sunshine-days.
I am being strong
and am moving on.

my beloved mommy

my beloved mom
when sunrise comes . . . i feel you
your sweet spirit shines

sometimes . . . i am lost
cries to hold you in my eyes . . .
mother's divine scent

a perfect rose . . . EyE
yearn for your gentle kisses . . .
i Love you so much_____.

Poetic Blossoms

I love poetic blossoms . . .
It's National Poetry Month
What a fantastic way to spread our wings and soar . . .
Writers, write on!
I love reading all of the wondrous creations . . .
That poets / poetesses share with the world
It's so wonderful to take such emotive journeys
Emotions felt sometimes bring sadness
At times, the writer evokes a romantic passion
Quite often, a reader is taken to new heights
No matter what the scribe is . . .
It's a universal piece of literature that can be shared
It's a work of art that can be felt by all

As a writer myself . . .
I adore the April Write Challenges!
I feel like an autumn flower blossoming

The poetic atmosphere fills me
It's fulfilling in many amazing ways . . .
I awaken to inspiration beyond this galaxy

At times, it's difficult to explain
One just has to be connected to this crazy intoxicating world
It's like an exhilarating carnival ride that you wish could go on a bit longer
It's like spending time with out of town friends / family and wishing they could stay
It's like meeting one's soul-mate and waking up together everyday
I love poetic blossoms . . .

My Hero

As I skirmish on the icy pew,

he no longer breathes the breath of origin.

The dust, still wavering;

delicate face vanishing,

a true being . . .

He strived to unite his brethren.

Though . . .

we have gathered to say goodbye,

I will always remember this gentle giant,

my Hero

*R.I.F. (Rest in Freedom) Dedicated to my beloved Father / Daddy, King Michael S. Jones Sr. I miss you & will love you 4Eternity.

A Legacy of Queen Matriarchs

Mother Earth . . .
Forgotten Spirits
Beautiful
Strong
Fierce
Women . . . Mothers . . . Sisters . . . Aunts . . .
I represent a legacy of Queen Matriarchs

Black . . .
Ebony . . .
Queen . . .
Lovin' me . . .
Just the way I am . . .
Unapologetic . . .
For my chocolate skin
Lovin' me . . .
and the skin I am in____.

Dedicated to My Ebony Queens

I am sending a lot of Love to you.
I know it is getting harder to paint on red lipstick
and smile behind tears;
our babies are not safe in this world filled with so much HATE.
I keep you uplifted in my prayers.
I do not know you all personally,
but i embrace you as my Queen Sisters.

Feel me . . .

Listen gorgeous Queens:
a queen resides in you all
can you hear her speak_____?
I Love You!

Truth

Sometimes . . .
atoms matter
explosions within
shake the temple
deafening ears
pierces mute
succumb to stillness
sit in your space
let the silence rest

Then . . .
pursue dreams
pursue desires
pursue needs

stay true to you____.

Tranquility

take me with you . . . love
tranquility becomes us
miss me . . . rising years
bathe in rosaries
floating in serenity
wash away death-fears

calm still waters . . . move
tranquility becomes us
glide through pain . . . black waves

painted sacred scenes
stroked cold floods . . . broken whispers
chasing spotlight . . . days

God-loving futures
hopes and dreams . . . buried crosses
Father . . . Mother earth

sun-sprouting splashes . . .
tranquility becomes us
one accord . . . first light_____.

*Inspired by my beloved Queen Sister, Lady Lisa aka Avel Eddy

My Love for Thee

Can we rise with grace
Even though liberty moves with eyes closed?
Hoping to un-see all of the damage done
Cheating government acting apprentice fame
Foreboding a state of more lies and disgrace
The enemy slithering orange, red and stolen gold
A country that wear hundreds of years shame

They . . .
Never hold the key

Stay the course, dear souls,
To eternity

Beautiful spirits,
Not those same heartbeats in vein,
They live by the sword

That is how they choose
To die a death with Satan
I always choose love
S/He is my savior
Without blindsight . . . EyE see thee
Taste my faithful kiss_____.
 I will always love thee.

Praying . . .

Mother earth . . . spirit,
nature is being destroyed.
Can you hear the call?

Babies are dying.
Streets filled with uniforms stained
innocent blood spills.

Who will stand with me?
Blues with silver badge lying . . .
spewing Christ their shield.

Hold on, my people,
love hard on those who love you.
Pray . . . restoration_____.

Breaking the Rules

there is no pain to show
i keep it locked away
in the back of my mouth
where my tooth aches
i might need an extraction

being alone has its rewards
like black and white
no harm in looking for grey
i learn the rules . . .
so i can break them
doing the right thing
may not always mean
doing the right thing
i do not run from problems
i was once told
to be glad i just had one
hmph_____!
i found humor there
sometimes love truly is blind

i love black
like i love silk and satin
like i love the idea of love and lust
like i love feathers and hard stiffness
like i love being used and useful

i love white
i like how it stands in juxtaposition
like flesh tones draped on black skin
with platinum smiling hairs

God's Radiance

i want to taste my muse
her cup runneth over . . . full
i touched pain in her chalice
but it was not empty
i want to punctuate her verses
and bathe her in sympathy
her beautiful blackness . . . kissed
black and white for me
and i broke the rules . . .
Again_____.

Technical Difficulties

you found me
bound . . .
chained and locked within
the midst of sin
happened

he thought . . .
she thought . . .
you thought . . .
temperament would give in
rebuke Him
and go with them

the stench
black
the red
rot
the smoke
pain
friends' mask

strong memories waiting to forget . . .
bloody resurrection
wanting to end this 'ish

abstruse
misuse
abuse . . .

subjected to horrors
that makes one call for earl
head spinning out of control
technical difficulties
this webbed world

God's Radiance

i stay
i do not play
lessons learned
positive energy
grounds me
i have fun
and i pray . . .

A Love & Peace-Prayer

i pray for love's seeds

i and EyE see a world . . . peace

heal us Sun . . . rise Sons_____.

adorn with culture

family heritage . . . Love

reach . . . and teach . . . our youth____.

The Warrior Queen . . .

don't stop the race
face those hurdles
get around them
jump over them
slide under them
use your magra . . .
fulfill your journey
hear your purpose
feel the course
you can do it
taste completion
next . . .
AmeriKKKa
Let freedom ring!
One Nation under God!
Not one nation under racists!

Beyond Illness

every day is a struggle
and so is life
every day is like
"running a marathon with the flu!"
i continue to run or walk or crawl
whatever i can do to keep going
i tell myself that i need to keep moving
it is the only way i know how to survive

there are so many things i still want to do
there are people i want to continue loving on
there are places i want to visit
there are sights i want to see
there are kingdoms i want to explore
right here on earth

i hope to get beyond illness
i need to live my best life despite it
my purpose in this land of the living . . .
is to be and do all that i can
i want to give more
i want to make a difference in this world
especially for our children
i believe we all need some sort of healing . . .

is it righteous to ask our Creator?
humbly i ask and pray
for our beloved Father God to help us all
whatever our need is . . .
mentally, emotionally, physically and / or spiritually

my LOVE for you and for myself . . .
helps to sustain my faith through difficult times
as i continue to heal beyond illness . . .

God's Radiance

i want my light to shine
tears . . . pain . . . bleed within
praying . . . fighting . . . mercy . . . grace . . .
sane . . . insane . . . flip-flop
dragon-slayer . . . not
He . . . relieves my ills immune
. . . system back to health
i kneel . . . gratitude
i knead . . . fortitude
taste his love . . .
through You.

my crown

beauty in my locks
my hair is my crown
no more creamy crack
my gift flows naturally down
curls can be worn in fact
but,
i love the versatility
of a Nubian Queen's hair
we once were told that our kinks stink
any hair would smell if it's not clean
but the lies were just to keep us from achieving
what some cannot
their hair cannot manipulate like this
please, my gorgeous queen sisters
don't buy into the stereotype
not to shine negativity on my beautiful Queen sisters that choose perms and other
    straightening vices
i'm just sayin'
we don't have to buy into the lies that our natural hair is not beautiful
remember, we can slay with any style
straight, curly, braids, weave etc.
but,
your own crown is worthy
just as you are
no filter necessary
when you choose to go natural
you are still a gorgeous goddess and queen
Shine on . . .

dare to listen to your own muse-ic

too much pain in a world full of hatred & bigotry
i seek solace in my muse-ic
i dance to my own tunes . . .
dare to be different
i doubt at this age i will ever conform to society's views of right & wrong
look at the current state of the so-called majority
dare to be different

i open my arms to welcome differences
call me alien
please do
my humanity will not rest peacefully in a broken tree
some trunks are not solid foundations
only need to keep recycling the same bullsh*t
but NO
not me . . .
i would rather be the black sheep
the one who will not run and hide under dirty sheets washed clean to please the masses
    brewing pots full of hate
NO . . .
not me . . .

i will continue to play my muse~ic
i will continue to dance to my own audible rules of Love and kindness and acceptance of
    difference

i gain peace within when i breathe the sounds of my ancestors . . .
i believe they too want the cycle of new
to break slave mindsets broken cries
can you taste their pleasure when broken limbs and leaves fall from trees?
they worry not!
another seed has been freed from mister
another seed is unleashed in a world where conformity and greed are the norm
dare to be different . . .
dare to be free . . .

dare to use the muse-ic within you to change the world-view of what is beautiful . . .
of what is right and wrong . . .
dare to break the chains . . .
dare to be all of you . . .
enjoying life's journey and your own beautiful unique
muse-ic
my outstretched arms will always welcome you . . .
just as you are . . .
i love you!

For My Ancestors

i will remain humble
but not silent
i will remain respectful
but reciprocation is necessary
i will continue to give homage to my ancestors
i will continue to pray,
but not to a religion killing God's children
i will pray to our Creator of all things and humanity
i will pray for the children who have had the light stolen from their eyes
i will pray for our elders who are bond by their captives; even for those who have no
    understanding about being still held captive like slaves
i will continue to pray for my loved ones,
family, eXtended family and friends
i will continue do my best to honor my ancestors
and my purpose for being here on earth
being human . . .
i know i fall short . . .
i am grateful to all of my loved ones who are patient with me,
as i continue to grow into wisdoms of old and new
i honor everyone in my social circle
i and EyE Love and adore you all
i am doing my best to live my best life
even in the face of evil and adversity
i know that in the end of it all
i will stand v-i-c-t-o-r-i-o-u-s-l-y
for you . . .
4U
and for YOU . . .
and for ME____ .

Scattered

scattered . . .

tears flowin' . . .
news of another beloved soul transitioned
i want to escape death valley's lair
i know life's circle comes full
i wish knowledge could help me now

i'm screamin' . . .
potent is this hurt feelin'
will this broken heart ever mend?
wish i could fly
i wanna travel with the wind
like birds in a pack
the wind always carries them

i'm cryin' . . .
on edge of the earth
feelin' consumed by mucho malo
sunrise services the day of her birth
worthy . . .
was she

i'm prayin' . . .
Master,
please comfort me

i'm releasin' . . .
diving blindly into heart's pulse
i feel summer
watching ice retreat
as the ocean freezes
will the sun become weak?

God's Radiance

i'm standin' . . .
in the midst
of a seasonal change
beautiful life's flesh gone
just as the sea-ice breaks up
against the horizon

i am scattered . . .

Lana Joseph

When I Found You . . .

I found pleasure in the quiet
I found pleasure in the stillness
I found pleasure in the peace
When I found you . . .
I found new pleasure in me
I found additional purpose
I found divine ease
When I found you . . .
I found footprints in love
I found psalms for my soul
I found purple for my heart
When I found you . . .

The Phenomenal One . . .
4.4.2018

phenomenal she
purple worn through stained skin red
her smile replaced tears

wise words inspired
butterflies left their cocoons
phenomenal she
accessed dying souls
mindsets grew compassion lives
phenomenal she

wash away blue fears
she knew why the caged bird sings
phenomenal she

shared beyond the moon
simple . . . straight . . . raw . . . no chaser . . .
"When someone shows you who they are,
believe them the first time."

phenomenal she!

tribute to a Queen,
Dr. Maya Angelou
I will always love you!
Happy Heavenly 90th B'Earth Day!

Brevity

I live here for now . . .

Needing . . . no separation

Love . . . our creator_____.

Brush strokes flowing . . . souls . . .

Painted masterpieces . . . pure

Only one savior_____.

Tasting Love's divine . . .

Touching art . . . she rose within

Beauty everywhere_____.

Ode to the Godfather of Soul

Brother King James Brown
Godfather of soul . . . singer
Dancer . . . inspires . . .

To date . . . this genius
Serves a divine gift of soul
Like no other man

Truth . . . he told
When he boldly shouted,
"Say It loud!"
"I'm Black and I'm proud!"

Yesss,
His legacy lives on . . .
This proud man lit the light of Love
Empowering brothers . . . stand
Empowering sisters . . . bond
Empowering children . . . pray

My beloved brothers and sisters . . .
Let's continue to Love, stand, bond and pray
We are One Creation . . .
Created and connected by One Divine Creator.

I will always Love you, Godfather of soul
Inspiring entertainer with a heart of gold
Thank you for your musical contributions
Historically, you are more than rock n' roll
Or a star on Hollywood's Walk of Fame
When your music is blasted on the radio
Even our youth responds to your name

*You will always be our Godfather of soul. Continue to RIP, beloved legendary King James Joseph Brown Jr. (May 3, 1933 - December 25, 2006)

No Need to Shovel the Sunrise!

Twenty and eighteen,
I said goodbye
Souls that could no longer remain
Lost loves that could not stay
No blind eyes turned
So many gone
Never forgotten
Twenty seventeen
One
Two
Three
Four
Five
Six . . . gone
Staying strong
Holding on
Legacy . . .

Yes!
Physically they are gone.
But,
I come from tribes unknown
Stolen lands
Still standing
Unknown family
Bloodlines . . .
Extensions
Heightened dimensions

Heritage . . .
Carrying pain and sorrow
Racial terrorism
Bearing burdens
Lies . . . greed . . . negativity
I do not envy
I no longer cry

God's Radiance

I wear wounds
And battle scars
Jealousy is no friend of truth
Holding hands with martyrs
Young and seasoned
Striving incessantly to just be . . .
She . . .
He . . .
Me . . .
Keeping family
Together strong

Focus not on expectations of others
Focus not on obligations of others
Focus only on authenticity
The first law of nature
Self-preservation

Make room for love
Respect peace and happiness

I cannot cry more
I hold the X Y and Z
I revere the alpha and omega
I am not a perfectionist . . .
There is . . .
No need to shovel the sunrise____.

That Place Within a Journey

Have you ever been at that place of the dead and undead?

That place in between

where you cannot see light at the end of the tunnel;

That place where you reach out trying to grasp for air,

while simultaneously hoping to capture the distorted smiles of yesteryears?

Knowing all the while

nothing you do will make up for innocent souls

who got caught up in the enemies' interned holes . . .

Lies and fear keep dancing tango with innocent lives

You know . . .

the children are the ones who always suffer

the most!

I'm a Natural Born Libra

It was already determined
when Father planted the seed in her
to Birth A Natural Born Leader

Leading in the hearts and souls of those
who will stand toe-to-toe just waiting
to get a glance at the most signature
balance

Chances not to be taken, which
by the way, not trying to get all wrapped up
into semantics . . .

But yes,
Libras can be desired romantics

Do not bury me deep into your heart
and then hide me in the dark
We are not sell-outs
but many of us get sold out

So, let me just spell it all out
L-Lover of Beauty
I-Idealistic
B-Balanced Realistic
R-Romantic Characteristic
A-Artistic Eclectic

Do Wop Do Wop Do Wop Do Wop . . .
Characteristics don't STOP
Sophisticated, kisses so wildly amazing
Peaceful dinners and relaxed star-gazing
and about intimate Love . . .
Well . . . let's just say,
Romantically, "Curtain Raising"

first kisses

like butterflies dancing in my stomach
i never knew the taste of love's lips
i have never been kissed by soul's comfort
anticipating our fun skinny-dips

nervousness cooled with warm hands felt
caressing soothing satisfying words, a b c
calmed this anxious Queen's anatomy melt
lips to lips pressed foreplay 1 . . . 2 . . . 3 . . .

i will never forget my first kisses
the ones that count brought me home
filled me up and made me the final Mrs.
a lifetime of kisses for Mr. on the throne

A Celebration

There are many things to celebrate.
Everything will return to
a celebration of love and life.

The air we breathe,
The sun, the moon and the stars,
The roof over our heads,
The food we eat,
The clothes we wear . . .
Everything is a blessing
and worth a celebration.
The best things and the worst
can be celebrated.

I was once told
"Things can always get worse!"
And . . .
"Never say Never!"
That one is old.
But . . .
it costs zero, zilch or nothing
to celebrate everything.

A celebration
of new life . . . new birth on earth . . .
Forward . . . never quit.

A celebration . . .
Transitions . . . new death on earth . . .
True love eXtends life . . .

But . . .
depending on one's perception,
there are many things
worthy of a celebration.

the brightly-lit light in their eyes

God Bless the child . . .
bright eyes illuminating . . .
sparkling like Christmas-tree lights
marveled in amazement
everything radiant and precious
and God-sent . . .
our most beloved gifts are being misused, abused and murdered
those stolen lives of innocent children can never truly be counted
there are too many faces
and too many names of those slain
for the melanin skin they live in
will Amerikkka's white eXtremists ever understand
that melanin skin is no crime?

will Amerikkka ever hold white eXtremists accountable
for their heinous crimes against our children?

those beautiful black and brown and white masterpieces . . .
will never breathe again
daily tragedies and travesties against our babies
are too painful for me to breathe at times
my heart continues to bleed as privileged enemies
refuse to see every sacred life
as a special human being . . . and beautiful living spirit
how long must our tears water the ground?
the violent transitions from earth are forever imprinted upon my heart and soul
they will never enjoy family, holidays, traditions, good times & bad
they will never shine as the beauty of a Rembrandt, Monet or Picasso
they will never be presented with opportunities or take daredevil chances

they will never visit the world of dreams . . . or create long lasting fun memories
they will never experience hard work or debate their disbelief in luck
they will never have true fierce-friends or meet new intriguing acquaintances
they will never grow old . . .

God's Radiance

that place in my soul where our Creator lives is where I visit multiple times
morning, day and night
I continue to pray for solutions
I want to believe that I can make a positive difference
if nothing more than to continue speaking out
continue staying vigilant watchful eyes wide open
leaving no room for another innocent baby to fall prey
if nothing more than to continue writing these truths
I need to believe that I can make a positive difference
I continue to pray for solutions
I visit that place in my soul where our Creator Father God resides

I will continue to visit multiple times
morning, day and night
hoping and praying I can help save our babies
I want so desperately to keep the beautiful brightly-lit light in their eyes

Just Me . . . Queen aka Lana "LJ" Joseph

i want to create a scribe that speaks soul to soul
smiles from within keeps my happy place fed
memories of the light in my little people's eyes
meeting mine every day
lined up waiting for me to greet them
with a resounding "good morning" or "good afternoon"

those days were truly "good times"
i felt doubly blessed by their eagerness
my young people wanted to learn
they were like sponges absorbing fluids
it was exciting to watch them grow
ravenously wanting to taste more knowledge

i was given children who were labeled
"rotten apples"
at first, i was shocked to know this revelation
soon, i realized ignorance on behalf of those adults
in my eyes, heart and soul
i was blessed
my students became my kids
challenging . . . yes . . .
though they were my labor of love
my gifts from our beloved Creator
i was staring in the faces of my new geniuses
i love all children
so, i rewrote their narrative about "my kids"

genius is common in my classroom
year one with my new students
(who were labeled before my arrival)
i worked very hard with them
and my kids were willing babies
they scored 51% on standardized tests
above all other classes
in the same ELA discipline

God's Radiance

no longer were "my children"
wearing inappropriate labels
placed on them by adults who could not see
blind . . .
no sight
nor insight
regarding "my shining brightly-lit lights"

some only focus on past grades
past actions
old instruction for all children
every child is uniquely bright and special
every child deserves an opportunity to learn
every child does not learn the same way
just as . . .
every child deserves to be loved

this scribe is for the thousands of children that i was blessed to teach
and doubly blessed to learn from . . .
i will always love you
thank you for loving me
thank you for trusting me
thank you for teaching me as well
i miss being in your divine presence
i am forever grateful for my classroom experiences
i hold you in my eyes
i hold you in my heart

our bond is love and respectful
divinely everlasting
soul to soul

i love you all . . .

Loving ME

Finally,
I have embraced my beauty . . .
My melanin skin
My love for all shapes
All sizes
Not give way to stereotypes of thin
Being the only way to win
Lovers and men
Who believe beauty is only on the outside
My brain . . .
And my social circle have no room for those mindsets
Thank God and Goddesses and my Ancestors
for allowing me to see truths among lies that have plagued my people . . .
Over and over again . . .
My melanin sisters and brothers
For waaaaay too long have been caught up in societies views about beauty
As my cousin cube says, "the new white is orange!"
Finally,
All chains are broken here
No slave mindsets in my circumference
No slave mindsets in my social circle
There is no room for those that can't look past their souls and express love instead of hate
After a while, the toxic air will consume us all if we choose that route . . .
Feel free to call it fate
That is your choice . . .
But, then again, I am just one woman
One queen
One goddess who has made a conscience choice to choose love over hate . . .
Good over evil
That is how I choose to use my free will!
How about you?
I Love You!

God's Radiance

When I look through my eyes,
I see what our heavenly Father needs me to see
Blackened street souls of evil beings
Washed away in His blood.

Yes . . .
Jesus, Yeshua, Yahweh . . .

I see wondrous visions . . .
Glory-filled earth
Lights beyond this world
Lit from above.

Yes . . .
God's perfect love,
As I sit breathing the breaths
Of God's perfect creations,
I understand the purpose of being still . . .

> Our Master
> Our Father
> Our Deliverer
> Our Protector
> Our Teacher
> Our Healer
> Our friend
> Our Beloved

I see clearly . . .
All that He has me to know
I know clearly . . .
All that He has me to see.

Lana Joseph

God's radiance transcends earth
His radiance transcends man & woman.

God's radiance is the air that I breathe
And He's my lit-light
For life.
God's radiance is here on earth . . .
And lives within me through rebirth.

God's Radiance

The Author's Quotes
&
Haiku-Poems

god within

dare to be yourself . . .
touch heartbeat's muse from within
feel moist lips . . . taste kiss_____.

Free Not . . .

Freedom will not ring
Until the day we see . . . blind . . .
Color beings . . . love ____.

God's Precious Gifts

Heavenly Father,
Tears shed for your babies . . . lost;
Sons . . . daughters . . . earth's gifts____.

Beyond Hurt

Wounds . . . bodies . . .. defaced
Dark Energy embraced . . . rules . . .
Struggle versus hope____.

Dads Matter

Shout out to dads . . . truth
You are relevant . . . to sons
Life for daughters . . . love____.

nature

water . . . life . . . matter
God's most precious gift to man
mother . . . matrix . . . love_____.

Soul's Delight

Transcendental . . . love
Black bold bombastic beauty
Soul's congruency_____.

The Symbol

Chains are broken . . .
Soar, our beloved artist
You are Home, Sweet Prince _____.

Sisterhood

Beautiful Sisters . . .
Variety of souls . . . shades . . .
Shadows . . . gifts . . . of Love

Purpose Fuel . . .

My purpose of life . . .
to live a life of purpose
God breathes Love . . . souls choose____.

Natural Sistahs

Earth . . . space . . . Sun . . . goddess
Queen . . . woman . . . matriarch . . . friend
Bond . . . sisterhood . . . Love____.

Baby Souls

soul of a newborn
sunrise . . . anew beginning
your Love . . . i adore____.

Reverence

Stunning Haitian Queen . . .
Angelic sounds . . . gift of songs
Calm souls resting home____.

The Seat of Souls

There are times when I gaze at the wonderment of life . . .
And EyE SEE God's most precious Gifts . . .
In the EyE of your souls.

Listen

The quieter . . . I
Hear His words . . . enact Love . . . self . . .
Change . . . human action___.

God's Gifts

sacred baby smiles . . .
you warm my heart and soul's core
God's children bring love.

Wings . . .

Belle Reine star . . .
Golden treasure . . . Lord's sunshine
Soaring wings of love____.

Life

LIFE is a GIFT
and a divine PRESENT
just breathe____.

Unconditional Love

I kneel before thee
holding your lit-light . . . soul bound
your love forsakes . . . none____.

strength

unseen faces bleed . . .
tasting ghost moans from beyond
erase this soul . . . not____.

U-B-U-N-T-U

Universal bond . . .
Sharing . . . connecting humans
We . . . win . . . with savior____.

Evolution

your smile kissed my soul . . .
it changed my world . . . thank you love
I choose to keep on_____.

Silence

In silence,
we can hear God,
and touch souls.

Mi Amore

bathing smiles hidden
earthly fields . . . aroma fed
saving souls succumb____.

Love's Light

liquids tainted . . . blind
no explanation . . . sunrise
collaboration____.

Nakupenda / I Love You

one by one . . . they come
beauty in all shades . . . loving
children . . . we must save____.

A Queen Nugget Soars . . .

To soar above and beyond expectations . . .
Tis a gift that only one can fiercely pursue
Giving up . . . is not an option.

For Jewels

I kneel . . . pray . . . love . . . bless . . .
Pain . . . goes . . . Life is for Living
My Love breeds strength . . . Jewels___.

*RIP & RIF (Rest in Freedom) with our ancestors, my beautiful Queen Sister Jewels. I will always love you! I miss you already, Queen Sis! God has another beautiful angel.

Options

Love, Muse and Music
EyE Love Variety . . . You?
Morning . . . Day and Night____.

To Know Thee

Know no bounds . . . fear . . .
Conquering all . . . disguise . . . strip
Dark corners . . . the Sun shines____.

We Are . . .

Kings . . . Queens . . . kiss my soul
I see love's radiant floods . . .
Lit-light spills from Quills____.

Lana Joseph

Beloved Great-Grandmother

I remember you
Grandmother . . . love . . . sweet . . . brave . . . bold
Soulful . . . ancestors____.

Victorious

When doves cry . . . love . . . them
Know that we are connected . . .
Each . . . and every . . . one____.

Freedom's Psalm

listening to drums . . .
love . . . beats . . . heart . . . soul . . . music
let's unite as one____.

Soulmate

he climbed in her heart
through love's winter-wet window
revealed his goddess____.

Love

Love is the answer
Shine your light on this planet
Like the sun on earth___.

Righteous

Smashing the red hues
Trails of mahogany blues
Not too young for truths____.

R.I.P.

A chilled window-frame
skeletons displayed, who cares?
I do. Hushed cries speak.

happiness

happiness is us . . .
Sun . . . life's eternal
savior . . . Kings and Queens_____.

legacy

adorn with culture
family heritage . . . Love
reach . . . and teach . . . our youth____.

Music Mood

Monday moods . . . jazzy
Red . . . yellow . . . and purple hues
Feel me . . . feeling you_____.

EyE Represent . . .

Light . . . and Sun . . . chores done
      Strange EyE captured my glance
            Stares at I . . . and Eye____.

Resurrection

Shaven lines . . . bronze trail
Queens danced for daughters' Lilies
Kings fell . . . into spring____.

Sisterhood Love

Sun . . . behind the veil . . .
      Sister . . . you are my hero
          Beauty . . . how are you?

heritage

I remember you
Grandmother . . . love . . . sweet . . . brave . . . bold
Soulful . . . ancestors____.

Heal Thyself

Heal . . . hands . . . reach yonder . . .
Faithful . . . trusting . . . forgiving . . .
Press upon frail flesh____.

Kings' Rise

chosen Kings will rise
united . . . power beyond . . .
freedom fighters stand____!

uplifting . . .

When change becomes real . . . Love
Comprehend all . . . watch sight fall
Tall . . . EyE stand . . . with Queens_____.

Life's Storms

Weathering the storms . . .
Enduring pain . . . holding reigns . . .
Humbly . . . reign again____.

Our Creator

God is Love . . . divine . . .
Fulfills all needs . . . no worries
Let go . . . let God . . . lead_____.

Live . . .

Enchanting wall . . . peace . . .
Nature's beauty . . . God-given
Hear . . . smell . . . taste life's joys_____.

Forever Sisterhood

Earth . . . space . . . Sun . . . goddess . . .
Queen . . . woman . . . matriarch . . . friend
Bond . . . sisterhood . . . Love_____.

Perspectives

When we change our perspective,
Always coming from love,
We begin to know our great power.

Hold on . . .

Hold on, beautiful
Queens, mothers, women, wives, friends . . .
Earth Mothers within___.

Queens

Uplifting all Queens
Can we embrace each other?
Love the Creator . . . Love the Son___.

For My Queen SisTars

Love You Queen SisTars . . .
I admire you . . . Feel me . . .
Goddess . . . Empress . . . Queens ___.

Down Days

not feeling quite well
still grateful . . . land of living . . .
rain or sunshine . . . Love _____.

Our Precious Gifts

Love the babies . . . safe
Keep them close to our hearts . . . soul
God's . . . precious . . . Love . . . gifts___.

Truth Speaks Within

Being strong . . . freeze veins
Feel the lies flesh tells . . . deal truth
Battle . . . heal . . . wars end___.

Nature

Kiss spring's captive bliss
Hold me raw in your eyes . . . eye . . .
Let me taste love's rain___.

Dedicated to Haiti

Peering out this view
Viewing destruction . . . Haitian
Breathing breaths of life___.

Oneness

Love . . . Peace . . . Music . . . God
Laugh and dance to soul's rhythm
Spirits UNITE . . . One___.

Illuminating Love

Savor bitter-sweet
Hallowed one is truly Love
Tasted tainted tongues____.

Touching Love

Goosebumps erupt
Love's light touch . . . caresses streams
The aurora spurts____.

Spirit Full

Dance within my dreams
Draw the shades . . . that cover me
Taste my ink spill's dry____.

God's Connection

Beauty and pain . . . touch . . .
Heart strings pulled . . . cotton . . . lace . . . silk
Souls connecting . . . Love____.

surrender

a tattered heart's tale . . .
stories surface . . . behind scenes
smiles broken . . . life's love___.

Lana Joseph

cleanse . . .

soft light . . . sunrise . . . rays
oceans . . .. lakes . . . rivers . . . ponds . . . deep
liquid splashes . . . wash_____.

Love's Peace

Vibrant glowing day
Dance upon life's perch . . . stay still
Peacefully with Love_____.

Love's Bond

always set a queen
upon her throne . . . where He . . . King
will present Love's flow

Soulmates

his path leads to her
hold on queens . . . due time
embrace light dark wings

Faith

Dear Lord gave choices . . .
Breathe faith . . . pray for King's sacred life
Birth to transition_____

no ceilings

possibilities . . .
replicas . . . layers' graphic
priceless dance . . . housed souls____.

Depth

My transformation . . .
Shifted . . . found speed in the wind
Time rushed home . . . sparks peak____.

Tasting Sunrise

Praying for you, love . . .
May your journey taste the sunrise
Inner-child . . . peace . . . feel____.

Tyme

Tyme will not always give time . . .

Epilogue

About the Author

Lana 'LJ' Joseph, aka Queen, is a prolific poet who magnificently and eloquently captures the inner spirit of her readers and audiences through her creative writings. She challenges thought processes and ideologies by tackling untruths of many diversified contents in order to bring forth realities and truth in many areas of her collective literary work. Joseph's poetic style is supple and poised. Yet, her creativity is ferocious, and her wisdom is fierce.

The author is a retired classroom teacher of English as a Second Language, Social Studies and Theatre Arts. Her primary passions are theatre, writing and working with children. She has written more than nine plays – all of which have been produced; composed dozens of short stories and hundreds of poems. Lana has been writing most of her life, yet she has been publicly sharing her literary scribes only for the last seven years. She was a featured guest on Spotlight on Jazz and Poetry Radio Show on October 25, 2015.

Lana 'LJ' Joseph attributes her inspiration to her beloved late mother. To date, her mother is the reason why the author continues to share her creative gifts with the world. She also cites as her source of influence the artistic gift of all prolific creative spirits with whom God has connected her. She feels completely honored and humbled by the support from her close friends, whom she considers her extended family.

Inner Child Press

Inner Child Press is a publishing company founded and operated by writers. Our personal publishing experiences provide us an intimate understanding of the sometimes-daunting challenges writers, new and seasoned, may face in the business of publishing and marketing their creative "Written Work".

For more information:

Inner Child Press

www.innerchildpress.com

intouch@innerchildpress.com

'building bridges of cultural understanding'

www.innerchildpress.com

www.ingramcontent.com/pod-product-compliance
Lightning Source LLC
Chambersburg PA
CBHW080459110426
42742CB00017B/2939